# POETICS OF RELATION

ÉDOUARD GLISSANT

# Poetics of Relation

*translated by Betsy Wing*

Ann Arbor

THE UNIVERSITY OF MICHIGAN PRESS

2010   2009               7   6   5

*A CIP catalog record for this book is available from the British Library.*

**Library of Congress Cataloging-in-Publication Data**
Glissant, Edouard, 1928–
   [Poétique de la relation. English]
   Poetics of relation / Édouard Glissant : translated by Betsy Wing.
   p.   cm.
   Includes bibliographical references.
   ISBN 0-472-09629-X (cloth : alk. paper). — ISBN 0-472-06629-3
(alk. paper)
   1. Martinique—Civilization—20th century.   2. Language and
culture—Martinique.   3. Nationalism and literature—Martinique.
4. French language—Martinique.   5. Creole dialects, French—
Martinique.   6. Martinique—Dependency on France.   7. West
Indies, French—Relations—France.   8. France—Relations—West
Indies, French.   I. Wing, Betsy.   II. Title.
F2081.8.G5513   1997
972.98'2—dc21                                                   97-6997
                                                        CIP

Translation of this volume was made possible
by a grant from the National Endowment for the Humanities
under its Fellowship Program for College Teachers
and Independent Scholars.

ISBN 978-0-472-09629-9 (cloth : alk. paper)
ISBN 978-0-472-06629-2 (alk. paper)

*for Michael Smith, assassinated poet*
*for the archipelagos laden with palpable death*

*Sea is History.*
DEREK WALCOTT

*The unity is sub-marine.*
EDWARD KAMAU BRATHWAITE

# Contents

# Translator's Introduction

## Betsy Wing

"Je bâtis a roches mon langage."
(I build my language with rocks.)
—Glissant, *L'Intention poétique*

The stumbling blocks of a translation frequently exist at its
most productive points. Their usual first effect is frustration
caused by obstinate resistance (on both sides), but, in their
ever-renewed demand for conjecture, these apparent obstacles can allow us to escape the cramped, habitual postures of
our own thought. This is the hoped-for reward of transla-
tors—whose first work is to be attentive, even hopeful readers—then, with as many premonitions of disaster as prospects
of opening possibilities within their own languages, they
must confront the task of making these new openings available to new readers.

All of Édouard Glissant's work, as a poet, novelist, play-
wright, or theoretician from the very beginning (*Les Indes*
and *Soleil de la conscience* [1956], *La Lézarde* [1959]) has been
concerned with exploring the possibilities of a language that
would be fully Antillean. Such a language would be capable
of writing the Antilles into history, generating a conception
of time, finding a past and founding a future. It would escape
the passivity associated with an imposed language of fixed
forms (French) as well as the folklore traps of a language that

is no longer one of material production, its vocabulary fixed because stagnant (Creole). This Antillean language would provide the means for this place and its people to relate to the world as one among equivalent entities. Carrying the work of other theorists of Caribbean self-formation, such as Fanon and Césaire, into new dimensions, Glissant sees imagination as the force that can change mentalities; relation as the process of this change; and poetics as a transformative mode of history.

In an early collection of essays, *L'Intention poétique* (1969), Glissant made it clear that he had no interest in rejecting the language he speaks (French); his purpose would be better served by actions within it, by interrogating it. By the passionate intensity of his way of being in this language, he would force the Other to know his difference. He repeatedly destabilizes "standard" French in order to decategorize understandings and establish new relations, so that the constant transformation always at work in any living symbolic system, passing into the particularity of Antillean experience, can form the vibrant grounds for a full and productive participation among world cultures now and in the future.

Throughout the body of his work Glissant has combined the discipline of analytical thought with a determined refusal to accept the logic of linear sequences as the only productive logic. For a country whose history is composed of ruptures, to accept this linearity would imply a continued blindness to its own crazed history, its *temps éperdu,* and acceptance of the Western European epistemological principles that claim this history as its destiny. The structure of *Poetics of Relation* is based more on associative principles than on any steady progress toward irrefutable proof; it is an enactment of its own poetics. Providing a sense of the new relations created in its language as a whole—its transforming ecology—was the greatest challenge for an American English version.

The first and most obvious difficulty is presented by particular incidents in which Glissant forces new word complexes to put forward concepts of major importance to his theory. The new phrases in French, of course, are just as likely to stop readers in their tracks as abruptly as they do in English. Indeed, this is Glissant's intent—to provide sudden contact with an unforeseen relation in language, not unlike the collisions between cultures that he sees as productive of Relation. The most acute need here is to provide the same level of clues in an American English as those existing in the first version—preferably a formula both elegant and concrete but undomesticated, not subject to common linguistic usage, a mental image ready to create a new connection. Glissant himself frequently sets the new term within its definition (though not necessarily at its first occurrence), letting context indicate the potential for expansion in its meaning. But the slightly changing contexts and Glissant's insistence that a single term serve in every instance created difficulties not presented by words in current usage, in which local solutions are usually best. An example of this is *agents d'éclat,* which I have consistently translated as *flash agents* (having rejected a long list of candidates such as *dazzlers, glamour mongers,* etc., as suiting only one or two occurrences). This phrase includes, but is not limited to, our category The Media, with all the implications of shallowness, dazzle, and hegemony that this implies for us. But, as always in *Poetics of Relation,* activity in a concrete world is important; physical notions of the dazzling, explosive power of this agency cannot be left out. Think: flash in the pan for shallowness, the strobing flash of momentary glamour, the news flash in a sound byte from our sources.

Glissant creates these metaphorical noun phrases to name the reality he sees emerging in the world. From the point of view of the Métropole (Real France), Martinique and the other islands of the Antilles can seem to be "dust-specks on the sea," as DeGaulle, looking down from a plane, is said to have described them. To become other than dust, aggregating their scattered and lost histories into a concrete presence in this world—this totality-world (*totalité-monde,* henceforth untranslated)—the Antilles must assert their dense, opaque, rock-hard existence, as do the noun-phrases Glissant uses to push at the limitations of French. Part of controlling the substance of one's future would lie in controlling its nomenclature.

*Agents-d'éclat* is a terse example of the merging of various discourses in Glissant's work. *Agents*—has resonance in everyday language (*agents de presse,* etc.) but also carries overtones of political agency. *Éclat* (and *éclater,* the verb) is frequently repeated throughout Glissant's poetry and prose. *Éclat* in the case of *agents d'éclat* has a somewhat prejorative sense. It is the sort of dazzle that can cause a people to lose its footing. In numerous other instances, however, it represents the sudden movement, the explosion onto the contemporary scene of "marginal" peoples, and the possible brilliance of their future. Always it is metaphorical and poetic.

Another word complex, the verbal phrase: *donner-avec,* relays the concept of understanding into the world of Relation, translating, contesting, then reconstituting its elements in a new order. The French word for understanding, *comprendre,* like its English cognate, is formed on the basis of the Latin word, *comprehendere,* "to seize," which is formed from the roots: *con-* (with) and *prendere* (to take). Glissant contrasts this form of understanding—appropriative, almost rapacious—with the understanding upon which Relation must be based: *donner-avec. Donner* (to give) is meant as a generosity of perception. (In French *donner* can mean "to look out toward.") There is also the possible sense of yielding, as a tree might "give" in a storm in order to remain standing. *Avec* both reflects back on the *com-* of *comprendre* and defines the underlying principle of Relation. *Gives-on-and-with* is unwieldy, but unfamiliar tools are always awkward.

Balking at the task of translation is a questionable practice for a translator, but, along with *totalité-monde,* certain of Glissant's coinages remain here in French.* In some cases, no

*Untranslated French words are further discussed in the notes to the text or glossary.

matter how they were rendered in English, short of writing a complete sentence at each occurrence, a significant portion of the sense was gone. The final judgment came down to the use value of the translated words, the *use* (not necessarily usual) of the sign in question. While the best of translations can impart new levels of meaning to common words, an additional layer of impenetrability is of little or no use.* Three related images of the world set forth by Glissant: *la totalité-monde, les échos-monde,* and *le chaos-monde,* have been left untranslated here, therefore, not only because of the inherent difficulty in translating them concisely but also because they function as neologisms—no more instantly acceptable in French than in American English; (though, following the same principle, the translation includes many dutiful, if not inspired, neologisms—for example, *flash agents,* etc.). More important, the problem lies in their structure, which cannot be duplicated in English. The article clearly modifies the first element (*la totalité, les échos, le chaos*), but the second element (*monde*) is not a mere modifier, as it would appear to be if the normal English reversal of terms took place (that is, *world-totality, world-echoes, world-chaos*). In fact, in this third instance all the implications of ordered chaos implicit in chaos theory would slip away, leaving the banality of world disorder. Nor are these guises of the world (the world as totality, etc.); they are identities of the world. The world is totality (concrete and quantifiable), echoes (feedback), and chaos (spiraling and redundant trajectories), all at once, depending on our many ways of sensing and addressing it.

From the beginning of the text, in addition to these compoundings, there are idiosyncratic usages that erupt and remain, assertively subsisting through repetition.** *Errantry*

---

*This is not entirely true. To a student of ideologies they surely mark interesting moments when the languages, as perceived by a particular translator, are mutually resistant beyond repair.

**Glissant's particular use of the words *langue* and *langage* as well as *imaginaire* is discussed both in the notes and glossary.

(*errance*) will be the first of these. Here Glissant stresses overtones of sacred mission rather than aimless wandering; *errance*, its ending linked for the contemporary reader with deconstruction's validation of *différance*, deflects the negative associations between *errer* (to wander) and *erreur* (error). Directed by Relation, errantry follows neither an arrowlike trajectory nor one that is circular and repetitive, nor is it mere wandering—idle roaming. Wandering, one might become lost, but in errantry one knows at every moment where one is—at every moment in relation to the other. This is a word in which Glissant's literary formation, his "high" culture voice, is particularly apparent. A word out of the past, it is retrieved for the use of a people weakened and oppressed as much by imposed cultural interpretations as anything else; so that it enters the spiraling, transformative mode of Relation, in which every voice can be heard and all can be said.

Brought at the age of ten to Fort-de-France, Glissant received the best of French colonial education at the Lycée Schoelcher, where Aimé Césaire was the "prof" of modern languages. Like other children in the colonies dependent on France, he too had to learn about "nos ancêtres les gaulois"—those spurious ancestors who had somehow buried the genetic ancestors in nonhistory. He also read the same "classics" of Western literature, probably encountering what he describes as the great book of Mediterranean intelligence, the *Odyssey,* at precisely the same moment in his development as every French schoolboy in the Métropole. And, like other intellectually promising youths in the 1940s, prepared to become "more French than the French," his own odyssey, his errantry, took him from Martinique to pursue education to its farthest reaches—the level of the *doctorat d'état*—in Paris.

Creole is Glissant's "mother" tongue but remains truly that—a language of intimacy and friendship. French, the language of empowerment in Martinique, is his "natural" (that is, culturally provided) literary language. But it is important to Glissant that he write a French different from the so-called standard French of the Métropole: one made supple by Creole, one ready to incorporate all the aspects of its formation, one cognizant of the history of the Antillean people and ready to imagine for them both past and future. His analysis of the problems in Martinique emphasizes the impact of widespread, active repression of those parts of the not-quite-lost history considered shameful (where the mulatto elite is still more likely to hark back to some imagined Carib ancestor than to its African heritage). But though the first rupture with history occurred at the Middle Passage with the imposition of slavery and the French language, retrieving the history it-would-be-possible-to-know does not mean refusing the imposed French—now unquestionably part of what is sought in a quest for cultural self-definition. Utilization, (*outilization*), tooling of the past to serve the present, is Glissant's work.

The word *errantry* has archaic overtones in English that, though not necessarily present in *errance,* do play an interesting part elsewhere in Glissant's writing. French readers of Glissant's work would have a very clear sense that his vocabulary was not entirely that of mainland France, that it was something particular, Antillean perhaps, and his use of archaisms would be one of the clues.* The classical definition listed in the dictionary is frequently the one that suits the context—the usage example will be from Racine or Corneille. This practice, while a mark of Glissant's classical French education, also bears traces of the isolation of the culture of Martinique. There are words still in use on the islands that have slipped from current usage elsewhere. They provide a certain formality of tone, which is frequently all I have been able to salvage of their effect in French, but the translation contains a few lurking archaisms drawn in general from the classics-burdened, educated U.S. South.

It is even more difficult to give any sense of the Creolisms

---

*A few examples of this are Glissant's use of the word *héler,* common enough in Martinique for "to call out"; or *roidissement,* an old form of *raidissement,* "stiffening"; or *convoyer,* meaning "to convey" more than "to convoy."

that are at work in *Poetics of Relation*. In the case of Creole words, only when there was some American idiom that did not trivialize Glissant's thought or lend it an air of the ridiculous did I attempt to mark the term with any particular effect.* Simply sprinkling his text with Creole words, however, would accomplish very little for Glissant. It is the structural elements of Creole that are most important to his project of creating a language adequate to Antillean experience. This Antillean French would not leave Creole to languish in folklore or preciosity but would use some of its working principles.

In Creole, as in the African languages that formed its syntax, the limits between classes of words are less watertight than in French. That is, a noun may work as a verb, or vice versa, without calling undue attention to itself.[1] Other contemporary writers have employed this practice to escape hypercoded language constructions and to stress the transformative nature of their own writing. The demiurgic voice of Glissant's "prof," the first great Martinican poet, Aimé Césaire: "I who Krakatoa . . . who Zambezi . . . " comes to mind.[2] Another writer of cultural transformation, Hélène Cixous, part of whose poetic praxis depends on canceling "fixed" barriers to empower women, also makes frequent use of this device.[3] Such crossovers play a part in Glissant's attempts to render French more supple. They also work as instances of *métissage*, a word whose primary use describes the racial intermixing within a colony and its contemporary aftermath but which Glissant uses especially to affirm the multiplicity and diversity of beings in Relation. On a larger

*Examples here would be: *d'un seul balan* (*Poétique*, 218). *Balan* is Creole for "soaring, flight, speed," etc., which the idiom "at one fell swoop" translated well; and *L'ici-là* (*Poétique*, 204), which has the sound of modernity we are accustomed to finding in French critical thought of the late twentieth century, but marked here by the directness of country speech: "this-here." A few Creole words remain untranslated but defined in the glossary. As Glissant remarked, "The English readers are going to know more than the French."

scale the inclusion of various sorts of writing—the familiar, the poetic, the hortatory, the aphoristic, the expository—without placing more value on one than another, works toward a similar synthesis.

Creole culture in Martinique still interrelates with the syncretic and oppositional practices of Vodou, in which the future may be influenced, among other ways, by *Vévés*, figures traced on the ground. Glissant is very attentive to textual geography: punctuation, markers, spacing. In all of his writing, including *Poetics of Relation,* this graphic element is important—much as one expects it to be in poetry. Vodou's rites of transformation project the world as it *should* be; Glissant projects language as it *should* be. Even his use of suffixes and creation of compound words with their ritual dash plays a part in this geographical writing.

Strategies of orality, present in Creole, continue to mark spoken French in Martinique and lend an oracular tone to Glissant's language. One word will unleash another through association or some deeper, almost subconscious logic into powerfully rhythmic sentences. The discontinuities in the text, the melding of discursive syntax with a language whose beat is punctuated by repetition and improvization (La Cité de Platon est pour Platon, la vision de Hegel pour Hegel, la ville du griot pour la griot" [*Poétique,* 208]), provide almost constant examples of this.

This oral tradition remains clearly present in the Creole proverbs and sayings that constitute the familiar wisdom of Martinique. These formulations exemplify continuity but in form are discontinuous. When this form is employed by a philosopher, it is referred to as "aphorism," and, when the surroundings of these discontinuous statements are lost in history, we think of them as "fragments." The section of *Poetics of Relation* entitled "That Those Beings Be Not Being," a sequence of oracular riddles, at first (and finally) leads to comparisons with Heraclitus, but the suitability of their structure to Glissant's project lies in its reproduction of one of Creole's most enduring aspects: the proverb form—memorable because it is concise, repetitious, rhythmic, and opaque. Though Creole may be based on a "succession of forgettings" (83), its formal structures can be used to induce memory.

Glissant's intent, finally, is to realize Relation in concrete terms—in which language is made of rocks and words and in which the future can be made to open for the Antilles by beating a time other than the linear, sequential order of syntax. Verb, noun, subject, object, are not fixed in their places because, in the words of Glissant, "in Relation every subject is an object and every object a subject."

## NOTES

1. *Dictionnaire Créole Français*, by Ralph Ludwig, Daniele Montbrand, Hector Pouillet, and Sylviane Telchid (Paris: Servedit/Éditions Jassor, 1990), 12.
2. Aimé Césaire, "Lost Body," *The Collected Poetry*, trans. Clayton Eshleman and Annette Smith (Berkeley: University of California Press, 1983), 243.
3. See Hélène Cixous, *The Book of Promethea*, trans. Betsy Wing (Lincoln: University of Nebraska Press, 1991), xi, 9.

# Glossary

> "**Glossary**: for readers *from elsewhere,* who don't deal very
> well with unknown words or who want to understand
> everything. But, perhaps to establish for ourselves,
> ourselves as well, the long list of words within us whose
> sense escapes or, taking this farther, to fix the syntax of
> this language we are babbling. The readers *of here* are
> future."
>
> —Édouard Glissant, *Malemort*, 231

(Words discussed in the introduction or notes are not
included here.)

**antillanité:** "A method and not a state of being," according to
Glissant. Contrast this with his idea of what *creolité* (creoleness) is about. *Antillanité* is grounded concretely in
affirmation of a place, the Antilles, and would link cultures
across language barriers. Dash translates this as
"Caribbeanness" in *Caribbean Discourse.*

**békés:** Creole word used originally to designate the white
planters but now also any of their (white) descendants in
Martinique.

**carême:** The dry season. Martinique has only two seasons: the
rainy season, *hivernage,* and the dry, *carême.*

**djobs, djobeurs:** Odd jobs and those who do them. These
words, derived from the English word *job,* designate the
widespread, marginal economy dependent on the scraps

and bits (of work and material) that no one in the more affluent sector wants.

**Gehenna:** A hell, a place of fiery torment.

**gommier:** Traditional sailboat still raced along the coast of Martinique.

**imaginary:** Glissant's sense differs from the commonsense English usage of a conception that is a conscious mental image. Furthermore, the now widely accepted Lacanian sense in which the Imaginary, the order of perception and hallucination, is contrasted with the Symbolic (the order of discursive and symbolic action) and the Real (not just "reality" but what is absolutely unrepresentable) does not apply. For Glissant the imaginary is all the ways a culture has of perceiving and conceiving of the world. Hence, every human culture will have its own particular imaginary.

**laghia:** A traditional dance that takes the form of a battle.

**Lamentin:** An industrial city in whose mangrove swamps Glissant and his friends played as children. The Lézarde River flowed, now trickles through, and the backfilled swamps are now developed into the airport of Martinique.

**mabi:** A drink made from *bois magi* (*Collubrina elliptica*) and the peel of mandarines.

**madou:** A sweet drink made with limes.

**manchineel:** A plant found growing side by side with the sea-olive on the beaches of Martinique. When touched, the fruit of the manchineel inflicts painful burns that the leaf of the sea-olive can heal.

**marronage, marrons:** The *marrons,* "Maroons," are the fugitive slaves, and *marronage,* originally the political act of these slaves who escaped into the forested hills of Martinique, now designates a form of cultural opposition to European-American culture. This resistance takes its strength from a combination of geographical connectedness (essential to survival in the jungle and absent in the descendants of slaves—alienated from the land that could never be theirs), memory (retained in oral forms and vodou ritual), and all the canny detours, diversions, and ruses required to deflect the repeated attempts to recuperate this cultural subversion.

**mornes:** The hills rising abruptly behind the Caribbean beaches in Martinique. Deeply forested in places still, they are the savage and life-preserving land in which the Maroons took refuge.

**Pitons:** The high, jagged, volcanic mountains.

**Quechua:** Amerindians of South America known for their obstinate silence.

**yole:** Traditional skiff used by Martinican fishermen.

**zouc:** Martinican dance music.

POETICS OF RELATION

# IMAGINARY

*Thinking thought usually amounts to withdrawing into a dimensionless place in which the idea of thought alone persists. But thought in reality spaces itself out into the world. It informs the imaginary of peoples, their varied poetics, which it then transforms, meaning, in them its risk becomes realized.*

*Culture is the precaution of those who claim to think thought but who steer clear of its chaotic journey. Evolving cultures infer Relation, the overstepping that grounds their unity-diversity.*

*Thought draws the imaginary of the past: a knowledge becoming. One cannot stop it to assess it nor isolate it to transmit it. It is sharing one can never not retain, nor ever, in standing still, boast about.*

I

# APPROACHES

*One way ashore, a thousand channels*

# The Open Boat

For the Africans who lived through the experience of deportation to the Americas,* confronting the unknown with neither preparation nor challenge was no doubt petrifying.

The first dark shadow was cast by being wrenched from their everyday, familiar land, away from protecting gods and a tutelary community. But that is nothing yet. Exile can be borne, even when it comes as a bolt from the blue. The second dark of night fell as tortures and the deterioration of person, the result of so many incredible Gehennas. Imagine two hundred human beings crammed into a space barely capable of containing a third of them. Imagine vomit, naked flesh, swarming lice, the dead slumped, the dying crouched. Imagine, if you can, the swirling red of mounting to the deck, the ramp they climbed, the black sun on the horizon, vertigo,

*The Slave Trade came through the cramped doorway of the slave ship, leaving a wake like that of crawling desert caravans. It might be drawn like this: ➤──❮ African countries to the East; the lands of America to the West. This creature is in the image of a fibril.

African languages became deterritorialized, thus contributing to creolization in the West. This is the most completely known confrontation between the powers of the written word and the impulses of orality. The only written thing on slave ships was the account book listing the exchange value of slaves. Within the ship's space the cry of those deported was stifled, as it would be in the realm of the Plantations. This confrontation still reverberates to this day.

this dizzying sky plastered to the waves. Over the course of more than two centuries, twenty, thirty million people deported. Worn down, in a debasement more eternal than apocalypse. But that is nothing yet.

What is terrifying partakes of the abyss, three times linked to the unknown. First, the time you fell into the belly of the boat. For, in your poetic vision, a boat has no belly; a boat does not swallow up, does not devour; a boat is steered by open skies. Yet, the belly of this boat dissolves you, precipitates you into a nonworld from which you cry out. This boat is a womb, a womb abyss. It generates the clamor of your protests; it also produces all the coming unanimity. Although you are alone in this suffering, you share in the unknown with others whom you have yet to know. This boat is your womb, a matrix, and yet it expels you. This boat: pregnant with as many dead as living under sentence of death.

The next abyss was the depths of the sea. Whenever a fleet of ships gave chase to slave ships, it was easiest just to lighten the boat by throwing cargo overboard, weighing it down with balls and chains. These underwater signposts mark the course between the Gold Coast and the Leeward Islands. Navigating the green splendor of the sea—whether in melancholic transatlantic crossings or glorious regattas or traditional races of *yoles* and *gommiers*—still brings to mind, coming to light like seaweed, these lowest depths, these deeps, with their punctuation of scarcely corroded balls and chains. In actual fact the abyss is a tautology: the entire ocean, the entire sea gently collapsing in the end into the pleasures of sand, make one vast beginning, but a beginning whose time is marked by these balls and chains gone green.

But for these shores to take shape, even before they could be contemplated, before they were yet visible, what sufferings came from the unknown! Indeed, the most petrifying face of the abyss lies far ahead of the slave ship's bow, a pale murmur; you do not know if it is a storm cloud, rain or drizzle, or smoke from a comforting fire. The banks of the river have vanished on both sides of the boat. What kind of river, then, has no middle? Is nothing there but straight ahead? Is this boat sailing into eternity toward the edges of a nonworld that no ancestor will haunt?

Paralleling this mass of water, the third metamorphosis of the abyss thus projects a reverse image of all that had been left behind, not to be regained for generations except—more and more threadbare—in the blue savannas of memory or imagination.

The asceticism of crossing this way the land-sea that, unknown to you, is the planet Earth, feeling a language vanish, the word of the gods vanish, and the sealed image of even the most everyday object, of even the most familiar animal, vanish. The evanescent taste of what you ate. The hounded scent of ochre earth and savannas.

"Je te salue, vieil Océan!" You still preserve on your crests the silent boat of our births, your chasms are our own unconscious, furrowed with fugitive memories. Then you lay out these new shores, where we hook our tar-streaked wounds, our reddened mouths and stifled outcries.

Experience of the abyss lies inside and outside the abyss. The torment of those who never escaped it: straight from the belly of the slave ship into the violet belly of the ocean depths they went. But their ordeal did not die; it quickened into this continuous/discontinuous thing: the panic of the new land, the haunting of the former land, finally the alliance with the imposed land, suffered and redeemed. The unconscious memory of the abyss served as the alluvium for these metamorphoses. The populations that then formed, despite having forgotten the chasm, despite being unable to imagine the passion of those who foundered there, nonetheless wove this sail (a veil). They did not use it to return to the Former Land

7

but rose up on this unexpected, dumbfounded land. They met the first inhabitants, who had also been deported by permanent havoc; or perhaps they only caught a whiff of the ravaged trail of these people. The land-beyond turned into land-in-itself. And this undreamt of sail, finally now spread, is watered by the white wind of the abyss. Thus, the absolute unknown, projected by the abyss and bearing into eternity the womb abyss and the infinite abyss, in the end became knowledge.

Not just a specific knowledge, appetite, suffering, and delight of one particular people, not only that, but knowledge of the Whole, greater from having been at the abyss and freeing knowledge of Relation within the Whole.

Just as the first uprooting was not marked by any defiance, in the same way the prescience and actual experience of Relation have nothing to do with vanity. Peoples who have been to the abyss do not brag of being chosen. They do not believe they are giving birth to any modern force. They live Relation and clear the way for it, to the extent that the oblivion of the abyss comes to them and that, consequently, their memory intensifies.

For though this experience made you, original victim floating toward the sea's abysses, an exception, it became something shared and made us, the descendants, one people among others. Peoples do not live on exception. Relation is not made up of things that are foreign but of shared knowledge. This experience of the abyss can now be said to be the best element of exchange.

For us, and without exception, and no matter how much distance we may keep, the abyss is also a projection of and a perspective into the unknown. Beyond its chasm we gamble on the unknown. We take sides in this game of the world. We hail a renewed Indies; we are for it. And for this Relation

8

made of storms and profound moments of peace in which we may honor our boats.

This is why we stay with poetry. And despite our consenting to all the indisputable technologies; despite seeing the political leap that must be managed, the horror of hunger and ignorance, torture and massacre to be conquered, the full load of knowledge to be tamed, the weight of every piece of machinery that we shall finally control, and the exhausting flashes as we pass from one era to another—from forest to city, from story to computer—at the bow there is still something we now share: this murmur, cloud or rain or peaceful smoke. We know ourselves as part and as crowd, in an unknown that does not terrify. We cry our cry of poetry. Our boats are open, and we sail them for everyone.

# Errantry, Exile

Roots make the commonality of errantry[1] and exile, for in both instances roots are lacking. We must begin with that.[2] Gilles Deleuze and Felix Guattari criticized notions of the root and, even perhaps, notions of being rooted. The root is unique, a stock taking all upon itself and killing all around it. In opposition to this they propose the rhizome, an enmeshed root system, a network spreading either in the ground or in the air, with no predatory rootstock taking over permanently. The notion of the rhizome maintains, therefore, the idea of rootedness but challenges that of a totalitarian root. Rhizomatic thought is the principle behind what I call the Poetics of Relation, in which each and every identity is extended through a relationship with the Other.

These authors extol nomadism, which supposedly liberates Being, in contrast, perhaps, to a settled way of life, with its law based upon the intolerant root. Already Kant, at the beginning of *Critique of Pure Reason,* had seen similarities between skeptics and nomads, remarking also that, from time to time, "they break the social bond." He seems thus to establish correlations between, on the one hand, a settled way of life, truth, and society and, on the other, nomadism, skepticism, and anarchy. This parallel with Kant suggests that the rhizome concept appears interesting for its anticonformism, but one cannot infer from this that it is subversive or that rhizomatic thought has the capacity to overturn the

11

order of the world—because, by so doing, one reverts to ideological claims presumably challenged by this thought.[3]

But is the nomad not overdetermined by the conditions of his existence? Rather than the enjoyment of freedom, is nomadism not a form of obedience to contingencies that are restrictive? Take, for example, circular nomadism: each time a portion of the territory is exhausted, the group moves around. Its function is to ensure the survival of the group by means of this circularity. This is the nomadism practiced by populations that move from one part of the forest to another, by the Arawak communities who navigated from island to island in the Caribbean, by hired laborers in their pilgrimage from farm to farm, by circus people in their peregrinations from village to village, all of whom are driven by some specific need to move, in which daring or aggression play no part. Circular nomadism is a not-intolerant form of an impossible settlement.

Contrast this with invading nomadism, that of the Huns, for example, or the Conquistadors, whose goal was to conquer lands by exterminating their occupants. Neither prudent nor circular nomadism, it spares no effect. It is an absolute forward projection: an arrowlike nomadism. But the descendants of the Huns, Vandals, or Visigoths, as indeed those of the Conquistadors, who established their clans, settled down bit by bit, melting into their conquests. Arrowlike nomadism is a devastating desire for settlement.*

Neither in arrowlike nomadism nor in circular nomadism are roots valid. Before it is won through conquest, what "holds" the invader is what lies ahead; moreover, one could almost say that being compelled to lead a settled way of life

---

* The idea that this devastation can turn history around in a positive manner (in relation to the decline of the Roman Empire, for example) and beget some fertile negative element does not concern us here. Generally speaking, what is meant is that arrowlike nomadism gives birth to new eras, whereas circular nomadism would be endogenous and without a future. This is a pure and simple legitimation of the act of conquest.

12

would constitute the real uprooting of a circular nomad. There is, furthermore, no pain of exile bearing down, nor is there the wanderlust of errantry growing keener. Relation to the earth is too immediate or too plundering to be linked with any preoccupation with identity—this claim to or consciousness of a lineage inscribed in a territory. Identity will be achieved when communities attempt to legitimate their right to possession of a territory through myth or the revealed word. Such an assertion can predate its actual accomplishment by quite some time. Thus, an often and long contested legitimacy will have multiple forms that later will delineate the afflicted or soothing dimensions of exile or errantry.

In Western antiquity a man in exile does not feel he is helpless or inferior, because he does not feel burdened with deprivation—of a nation that for him does not yet exist. It even seems, if one is to believe the biographies of numerous Greek thinkers including Plato and Aristotle, that some experience of voyaging and exile is considered necessary for a being's complete fulfillment. Plato was the first to attempt to base legitimacy not on community within territory (as it was before and would be later) but on the City in the rationality of its laws. This at a time when his city, Athens, was already threatened by a "final" deregulation.*

In this period identification is with a culture (conceived of as civilization), not yet with a nation.** The pre-Christian West along with pre-Columbian America, Africa of the time of the great conquerors, and the Asian kingdoms all shared this mode of seeing and feeling. The relay of actions exerted

*Platonic Dialogues take over the function of the Myth. The latter establishes the legitimacy of the possession of a territory based usually on the uninterrupted rigors of filiation. The Dialogue establishes the City's justice based on the revelation of a superior reason organizing rigorous successions of a political order.
**Through the entirely Western notion of civilization the experience of a society is summed up, in order to project it immediately into an evolution, most often an expansion as well. When one says civilization, the immediate implication is a will to civilize. This idea is linked to the passion to impose civilization on the Other.

by arrowlike nomadism and the settled way of life were first directed against generalization (the drive for an identifying universal as practiced by the Roman Empire). Thus, the particular resists a generalizing universal and soon begets specific and local senses of identity, in concentric circles (provinces then nations). The idea of civilization, bit by bit, helps hold together opposites, whose only former identity existed in their opposition to the Other.

During this period of invading nomads the passion for self-definition first appears in the guise of personal adventure. Along the route of their voyages conquerors established empires that collapsed at their death. Their capitals went where they went. "Rome is no longer in Rome, it is wherever I am." The root is not important. Movement is. The idea of errantry, still inhibited in the face of this mad reality, this too-functional nomadism, whose ends it could not know, does not yet make an appearance. Center and periphery are equivalent. Conquerors are the moving, transient root of their people.

The West, therefore, is where this movement becomes fixed and nations declare themselves in preparation for their repercussions in the world. This fixing, this declaration, this expansion, all require that the idea of the root gradually take on the intolerant sense that Deleuze and Guattari, no doubt, meant to challenge. The reason for our return to this episode in Western history is that it spread throughout the world. The model came in handy. Most of the nations that gained freedom from colonization have tended to form around an idea of power—the totalitarian drive of a single, unique root—rather than around a fundamental relationship with the Other. Culture's self-conception was dualistic, pitting citizen against barbarian. Nothing has ever more solidly opposed the thought of errantry than this period in human history when Western nations were established and then made their impact on the world.

At first this thought of errantry, bucking the current of nationalist expansion, was disguised "within" very personalized adventures—just as the appearance of Western nations had been preceded by the ventures of empire builders. The errantry of a troubadour or that of Rimbaud is not yet a thorough, thick (opaque) experience of the world, but it is already an arrant, passionate desire to go against a root. The reality of exile during this period is felt as a (temporary) lack that primarily concerns, interestingly enough, language. Western nations were established on the basis of linguistic intransigence, and the exile readily admits that he suffers most from the impossibility of communicating in his language. The root is monolingual. For the troubadour and for Rimbaud errantry is a vocation only told via detour. The call of Relation is heard, but it is not yet a fully present experience.

However, and this is an immense paradox, the great founding books of communities, the Old Testament, the *Iliad,* the *Odyssey,* the *Chansons de Geste,* the Islandic *Sagas,* the *Aeneid,* or the African epics, were all books about exile and often about errantry. This epic literature is amazingly prophetic. It tells of the community, but, through relating the community's apparent failure or in any case its being surpassed, it tells of errantry as a temptation (the desire to go against the root) and, frequently, actually experienced. Within the collective books concerning the sacred and the notion of history lies the germ of the exact opposite of what they so loudly proclaim. When the very idea of territory becomes relative, nuances appear in the legitimacy of territorial possession. These are books about the birth of collective consciousness, but they also introduce the unrest and suspense that allow the individual to discover himself there, whenever he himself becomes the issue. The Greek victory in the *Iliad* depends on trickery; Ulysses returns from his Odyssey and is recognized only by his dog; the Old Testament David bears the stain of adultery and murder; the *Chanson de Roland* is the chronicle of a defeat; the characters in the *Sagas* are branded by an unstemmable fate, and so forth. These books are the begin-

15

ning of something entirely different from massive, dogmatic, and totalitarian certainty (despite the religious uses to which they will be put). These are books of errantry, going beyond the pursuits and triumphs of rootedness required by the evolution of history.

Some of these books are devoted entirely to the supreme errantry, as in the Egyptian Book of the Dead. The very book whose function is to consecrate an intransigent community is already a compromise, qualifying its triumph with revelatory wanderings.*

In both *L'Intention poétique* (*Poetic Intention*) and *Le Discours antillais* (*Caribbean Discourse*)—of which the present work is a reconstituted echo or a spiral retelling—I approached this dimension of epic literature. I began wondering if we did not still need such founding works today, ones that would use a similar dialectics of rerouting,[4] asserting, for example, political strength but, simultaneously, the rhizome of a multiple relationship with the Other and basing every community's reasons for existence on a modern form of the sacred, which would be, all in all, a Poetics of Relation.**

This movement, therefore (one among others, equally important, in other parts of the world), has led from a primordial nomadism to the settled way of life of Western nations then to Discovery and Conquest, which achieved a final, almost mystical perfection in the Voyage.

In the course of this journey identity, at least as far as the Western peoples who made up the great majority of voyagers, discoverers, and conquerors were concerned, consolidates

*Hegel, in book 3 of his *Aesthetics,* shows how the founding works of communities appear spontaneously at the moment in which a still naive collective consciousness reassures itself about its own legitimacy, or, not to mince words: about its right to possess a land. In this sense Epic thought is close to that of Myth.

**The necessary surpassing of mythic and epic thought took place in the political reason organizing the City. Epic expression is obscure and unfathomable, one of the conditions of naïveté. Political discourse is obvious. Surpassing can be contradiction.

16

itself implicitly at first ("my root is the strongest") and then is explicitly exported as a value ("a person's worth is determined by his root").* The conquered or visited peoples are thus forced into a long and painful quest after an identity whose first task will be opposition to the denaturing process introduced by the conqueror. A tragic variation of a search for identity. For more than two centuries whole populations have had to assert their identity in opposition to the processes of identification or annihilation triggered by these invaders. Whereas the Western nation is first of all an "opposite,"** for colonized peoples identity will be primarily "opposed to"—that is, a limitation from the beginning. Decolonization will have done its real work when it goes beyond this limit.

The duality of self-perception (one is citizen or foreigner) has repercussions on one's idea of the Other (one is visitor or visited; one goes or stays; one conquers or is conquered). Thought of the Other cannot escape its own dualism until the time when differences become acknowledged. From that point on thought of the Other "comprehends"[5] multiplicity, but mechanically and still taking the subtle hierarchies of a generalizing universal as its basis. Acknowledging differences does not compel one to be involved in the dialectics of their totality. One could get away with: "I can acknowledge your difference and continue to think it is harmful to you. I can think that my strength lies in the Voyage (I am making History) and that your difference is motionless and silent." Another step remains to be taken before one really enters the dialectic of totality. And, contrary to the mechanics of the Voyage, this dialectic turns out to be driven by the thought of errantry.

*That is, as we have said, essentially by his language.
**If the idea of civilization holds opposites together, a generalizing universal will be the principle of their action in the world, the principle that will allow them to realize conflicts of interest in a finalist conception of History. The first colonist, Christopher Columbus, did not voyage in the name of a country but of an idea.

Let us suppose that the quest for totality, starting from a nonuniversal context of histories of the West, has passed through the following stages:

—the thinking of territory and self (ontological, dual)
—the thinking of voyage and other (mechanical, multiple)
—the thinking of errantry and totality (relational, dialectical).

We will agree that this thinking of errantry, this errant thought, silently emerges from the destructuring of compact national entities that yesterday were still triumphant and, at the same time, from difficult, uncertain births of new forms of identity that call to us.

In this context uprooting can work toward identity, and exile can be seen as beneficial, when these are experienced as a search for the Other (through circular nomadism) rather than as an expansion of territory (an arrowlike nomadism). Totality's imaginary allows the detours that lead away from anything totalitarian.

Errantry, therefore, does not proceed from renunciation nor from frustration regarding a supposedly deteriorated (deterritorialized) situation of origin; it is not a resolute act of rejection or an uncontrolled impulse of abandonment. Sometimes, by taking up the problems of the Other, it is possible to find oneself. Contemporary history provides several striking examples of this, among them Frantz Fanon, whose path led from Martinique to Algeria. That is very much the image of the rhizome, prompting the knowledge that identity is no longer completely within the root but also in Relation. Because the thought of errantry is also the thought of what is relative, the thing relayed as well as the thing related. The thought of errantry is a poetics, which always infers that at some moment it is told. The tale of errantry is the tale of Relation.

18

In contrast to arrowlike nomadism (discovery or conquest), in contrast to the situation of exile, errantry gives-on-and-with the negation of every pole and every metropolis, whether connected or not to a conqueror's voyaging act. We have repeatedly mentioned that the first thing exported by the conqueror was his language. Moreover, the great Western languages were supposedly vehicular languages, which often took the place of an actual metropolis. Relation, in contrast, is spoken multilingually. Going beyond the impositions of economic forces and cultural pressures, Relation rightfully opposes the totalitarianism of any monolingual intent.

At this point we seem to be far removed from the sufferings and preoccupations of those who must bear the world's injustice. Their errantry is, in effect, immobile. They have never experienced the melancholy and extroverted luxury of uprooting. They do not travel. But one of the constants of our world is that a knowledge of roots will be conveyed to them from within intuitions of Relation from now on. Traveling is no longer the locus of power but, rather, a pleasurable, if privileged, time. The ontological obsession with knowledge gives way here to the enjoyment of a relation; in its elementary and often caricatural form this is tourism. Those who stay behind thrill to this passion for the world shared by all. Or, indeed, they may suffer the torments of internal exile.

I would not describe the physical situation of those who suffer the oppression of an Other within their own country, such as the blacks in South Africa, as internal exile. Because the solution here is visible and the outcome determined; force alone can oppose this. Internal exile strikes individuals living where solutions concerning the relationship of a community to its surroundings are not, or at least not yet, consented to by this community as a whole. These solutions, precariously outlined as decisions, are still the prerogative of only a few, who, as a result, are marginalized. Internal exile is the voyage out of this enclosure. It is a motionless and exacerbated introduction to the thought of errantry. Most often it is diverted into partial, pleasurable compensations in which the individual is consumed. Internal exile tends toward material comfort, which cannot really distract from anguish.

Whereas exile may erode one's sense of identity, the thought of errantry—the thought of that which relates—usually reinforces this sense of identity. It seems possible, at least to one observer, that the persecuted errantry, the wandering of the Jews, may have reinforced their sense of identity far more than their present settling in the land of Palestine. Being exiled Jews turned into a vocation of errantry, their point of reference an ideal land whose power may, in fact, have been undermined by concrete land (a territory), chosen and conquered. This, however, is mere conjecture. Because, while one can communicate through errantry's imaginary vision, the experiences of exiles are incommunicable.

The thought of errantry is not apolitical nor is it inconsistent with the will to identity, which is, after all, nothing other than the search for a freedom within particular surroundings. If it is at variance with territorial intolerance, or the predatory effects of the unique root (which makes processes of identification so difficult today), this is because, in the poetics of Relation, one who is errant (who is no longer traveler, discoverer, or conqueror) strives to know the totality of the world yet already knows he will never accomplish this—and knows that is precisely where the threatened beauty of the world resides.

Errant, he challenges and discards the universal—this generalizing edict that summarized the world as something obvious and transparent, claiming for it one presupposed sense and one destiny. He plunges into the opacities of that part of the world to which he has access. Generalization is totalitarian: from the world it chooses one side of the reports, one set of ideas, which it sets apart from others and tries to impose by exporting as a model. The thinking of errantry conceives of totality but willingly renounces any claims to sum it up or to possess it.

The founding books have taught us that the sacred dimension consists always of going deeper into the mystery of the root, shaded with variations of errantry. In reality errant thinking is the postulation of an unyielding and unfading sacred. We remember that Plato, who understood the power of Myth, had hoped to banish the poets, those who force obscurity, far from the Republic. He distrusted the fathomless word. Are we not returning here, in the unforeseeable meanders of Relation, to this abyssal word? Nowhere is it stated that now, in this thought of errantry, humanity will not succeed in transmuting Myth's opacities (which were formerly the occasion for setting roots) and the diffracted insights of political philosophy, thereby reconciling Homer and Plato, Hegel and the African griot.

But we need to figure out whether or not there are other succulencies of Relation in other parts of the world (and already at work in an underground manner) that will suddenly open up other avenues and soon help to correct whatever simplifying, ethnocentric exclusions may have arisen from such a perspective.

*

As far as literature is concerned (without my having to establish a pantheon, an isolation these works would refuse), there are two contemporary bodies of work, it seems to me, in which errantry and Relation are at play.

Faulkner's work, somehow theological. This writing is about digging up roots in the South—an obvious place to do so in the United States. But the root begins to act like a rhizome; there is no basis for certainty; the relation is tragic. Because of this dispute over source, the sacred—but henceforth unspeakable—enigma of the root's location, Faulkner's

21

world represents one of the thrilling moments in the modern poetics of Relation. At one time I regretted that such a world had not gone farther, spreading its vision into the Caribbean and Latin America. But, perhaps, this was a reaction of unconscious frustration on the part of one who felt excluded.

And Saint-John Perse's erratic work, in search of that which moves, of that which goes—in the absolute sense.[6] A work leading to totality—to the out-and-out exaltation of a universal that becomes exhausted from being said too much.

# Poetics

In the nineteenth century, after the Spanish language had expanded into South America and the Portuguese language into Brazil, the French and English languages successfully accompanied the widespread expansion of their own respective cultures around the world. Other Western languages, German, Italian, or Russian, for example, despite some limited attempts at colonization, were not driven by this propensity for self-exportation that nearly always generates a sort of vocation for the universal. As for non-Western languages, Quechua, Swahili, Hindi, or Chinese, they remain endogenous and nonproliferating; their poetics do not yet hint at involvement in the evolution of world histories.

Our aim here is to advance the notion that, within the limited framework of one language—French—competing to discover the world and dominate it, literary production is partly determined by this discovery, which also transforms numerous aspects of its poetics; but that there persists, at least as far as French is concerned, a stubborn resistance to any attempt at clarifying the matter. Everything just goes along as if, at the moment it entered into the poetics of worldwide Relation, ready to replace the former hegemony, collective thought working within the language chose to cover up its expressive relationship with the other, rather than admit any participation that would not be one of preeminence.

With generally good results literary theoreticians have been content to define the poetics deemed responsible for

23

the entrance of French literature into modernity beginning in the nineteenth century. A theory of depth, a practice of language-in-itself, and the problematics of textual structure were thus formulated. (I simplify for effect, to critical extremes.) They have pretended to forget that, in literature, just like everywhere else in the world, one of the full-senses[1] of modernity is provided henceforth by the action of human cultures' identifying one another for their mutual transformation.

Poetics of depth. Baudelaire explored the early realms of this form of poetics. The vertiginous extension, not out into the world but toward the abysses man carries within himself. Western man essentially, that is, who at that moment in time governed the evolution of modernity and provided its rhythm. Inner space is as infinitely explorable as spaces of the earth. At the same time as he discovered the numerous varieties of the species man constituted, he felt that the alleged stability of knowledge led nowhere and that all he would ever know of himself was what he made others know. As a result, Baudelaire quashed romantic lyricism's claim that the poet was the introspective master of his joys or sorrows; and that it was in his power to draw clear, plain lessons from this that would benefit everyone. This romantic beatitude was swept away by the stenches inseparable from Baudelairean carrion.

Poetics of depth—like depth psychology—does not, however, renounce its certainty that there is a universal model, a sort of archetype of humanity, difficult to circumscribe or define, of course, but one that would simultaneously ensure our knowledge in the matter and be its ultimate aim. These both tended, on the other hand, to displace the terrain of this knowledge: first dispossessing it of the sovereign subject (requiring the knowledge—the gaze, or the hearing—of another) then surrendering it to this subject (speaking "in" the structures of any expressed knowledge).

A poetics of language-in-itself. It sanctions the moment when language, as if satisfied with its perfection, ceases to take for its object the recounting of its connection with particular surroundings, to concentrate solely upon its fervor to exceed its limits and reveal thoroughly the elements composing it—solely upon its engineering skill with these. This practice does not proceed without rambling, because rambling—as Mallarmé well knew—is an absolute challenge to narrative. Rather than discovering or telling about the world, it is a matter of producing an equivalent, which would be the Book, in which everything would be said, without anything's being reported.* Mallarmé, who experienced, of course, the temptations of elsewhere, spent his energy solely on producing this totality of language. The world as book, the Book as world. His heroism within confinement is a way of celebrating a desired, dreamt-of totality within the absolute of the word.

The poetics of language-in-itself strives toward a knowledge that by definition would only be exercised within the limits of a given language. It would renounce (Mallarmé notwithstanding, with his anxious pleasure in being professor and translator of English) the nostalgia for other languages—for the infinite possible languages—now germinating in every literature.

A poetics of structure. The creator of a text is effaced, or, rather, is done away with, to be revealed in the texture of his creation. Just as narrative had been eliminated from Mallarméan poetics, History (in the sense given by the West to this word) must be considered in context, according to the structuralists. Emphasizing one more renunciation, a subtle one, of the world as it produces itself, that is, as it rightfully escapes the control of Western discoverers: explorers, merchants, conquerors, ethnologists—those men of intelligence, faith, and law.

*My intent in *Caribbean Discourse* was to question this equivalence.

25

The neutral rather than harsh actuality of the object; the tightening of a locus; the low regard for any thought claiming falsely to be final; the literal and the flat—these are a few of the factors linked with the works of numerous contemporary French authors that provide access to them within the context of this poetics.

Those involved with the exegesis of French literature since romanticism have looked to poetics of depth, science of language, and textual disclosure, in turn, for the authority to outline its problematics. But there is yet another—unnoticed, or rather evaded—that we shall call a poetics of Relation.

The cultures of the world have always maintained relations among themselves that were close or active to varying degrees, but it is only in modern times that some of the right conditions came together to speed up the nature of these connections.

The vague feeling that the end of the world had been reached, in the geographical sense, removed whatever element of adventure and perhaps blind belief there had been in the discovery of the other. Since the beginning of this century the shrinking of unexplored regions on the map of the world has made minds less infatuated with adventure, or less sensitive to its beauty, inclining more toward a concern for the truth of human beings. Understanding cultures then became more gratifying than discovering new lands. Western ethnography was structured on the basis of this need. But we shall perhaps see that the verb *to understand* in the sense of "to grasp" [*comprendre*] has a fearsome repressive meaning here.

Contacts among cultures—one of the givens of modernity—will no longer come across the huge spans of time that have historically allowed meetings and interchanges to be active but almost imperceptibly so. Whatever happens elsewhere has immediate repercussions here. Not long ago cultural influences were initially of a general nature, affecting communities progressively; today the individual, without having to go anywhere, can be directly touched by things elsewhere, sometimes even before his community, family, social group, or nation has been enriched by the same effect. This immediate and fragmentary repercussion on individuals, as individuals, permitted the premonitions of Victor Segalen or Raymond Roussel or the Douanier Rousseau—the first poets of Relation.

Finally—the third condition—the consciousness of Relation became widespread, including both the collective and the individual. We "know" that the Other is within us and affects how we evolve as well as the bulk of our conceptions and the development of our sensibility. Rimbaud's "I is an other" is literal in terms of history. In spite of ourselves, a sort of "consciousness of consciousness" opens us up and turns each of us into a disconcerted actor in the poetics of Relation.

Starting from the moment that cultures, lands, men, and women were no longer there to discover but to know, Relation represented an absolute (that is, a totality finally sufficient to itself) that, paradoxically, set us free from the absolute's intolerances.

To the extent that our consciousness of Relation is total, that is, immediate and focusing directly upon the realizable totality of the world, when we speak of a poetics of Relation, we no longer need to add: relation between what and what? This is why the French word *Relation,* which functions somewhat like an intransitive verb, could not correspond, for example, to the English term *relationship.*

We have already said that Relation informs not simply what is relayed but also the relative and the related. Its always approximate truth is given in a narrative. For, though the world is not a book, it is nonetheless true that the silence of the world would, in turn, make us deaf. Relation, driving humanities chaotically onward, needs words to publish itself, to continue. But because what it relates, in reality, proceeds from no absolute, it proves to be the totality of relatives, put in touch and told.

It is not merely a pleasant option to consider this "movement" within the context of French literature. Quite simply, two conditions have come together here: a culture that projected onto the world (with the aim of dominating it) and a language that was presented as universal (with the aim of providing legitimacy to the attempt at domination). These two intentions, not without some acknowledged portion of largesse, culminated in the thought of an empire.* Under these conditions poetic thought went on the alert: beneath the fantasy of domination it sought the really livable world.

It projected toward. As if it set out all over again on the trajectory of an earlier arrowlike nomadism. Moreover, the movements of this poetics can be located in space as trajectories, their poetic import being aimed at completing these trajectories in order to abolish them. These trajectories link the places of the world into a whole made up of peripheries, which are listed in function of a Center.**

The first of these trajectories led from the Center toward

*The empire is the absolute manifestation of totality. The thought of empire is selective: what it brings to the universal is not the quantity of totality that has been realized but a quality that it represents as the Whole. The empire thus usually attempts to forestall conflicts throughout its territory. But imperial peace is the true death of Relation.
**I outlined this route in _L'intention poétique:_ "From the One to the Universe—From the diverse to the common—The we of the other—The other of us." In _La lézarde,_ to evaluate our alienations, I mentioned the perspective of a Center for the first time.
    M. Samir Amin developed a global theory of worldwide economy, articulated in Centers (to produce and control) and Peripheries (to receive). He concluded that it was necessary for these peripheries to have a self-centered economy, proceeding from a will for "deconnection" in relation to the global system.

the peripheries. I take the work of Victor Segalen as an innovative example of this; but is it necessary to mention all those who, whether critical or possessed, racist or idealist, frenzied or rational, have experienced passionately the call of Diversity since his time: from Cendrars to Malraux, from Michaux to Artaud, from Gobineau to Céline, from Claudel to Michel Leiris?

A second itinerary then began to form, this time from peripheries toward the Center. Poets who were born or lived in the elsewhere dream of the source of their imaginary constructs and, consciously or not, "make the trip in the opposite direction," struggling to do so. Jules Supervielle. Saint-John Perse. Georges Schéhadé.

In a third stage the trajectory is abolished; the arrowlike projection becomes curved. The poet's word leads from periphery to periphery, and, yes, it reproduces the track of circular nomadism; that is, it makes every periphery into a center; furthermore, it abolishes the very notion of center and periphery. All of this germinated in the works of writers such as Segalen, Kateb Yacine, Cheik Anta Diop, Léon Gontran Damas, and many others it would be impossible to name.

The time came, then, in which Relation was no longer a prophecy made by a series of trajectories, itineraries that followed or thwarted one another. By itself and in itself Relation exploded like a network inscribed within the sufficient totality of the world.

Segalen's crucial idea was that encountering the Other superactivates poetic imagination and understanding. Of course, from that moment on there could be no question of hierarchy in pursuit of relations with the other. Let me point out, however, that Segalen does not merely describe recognition of the other as a moral obligation (which would be a banality) but he considers it an aesthetic constituent, the first edict of a real poetics of Relation. The power to experience

29

the shock of elsewhere is what distinguishes the poet. Diversity, the quantifiable totality of every possible difference, is the motor driving universal energy, and it must be safeguarded from assimilations, from fashions passively accepted as the norm, and from standardized customs.

Segalen wrote novels that are at the same time ethnological studies, declarations, and defenses; he struggled to explain the thought processes of Gauguin (in this instance his double); he projected also the main lines of a theoretical essay on exoticism, considered as an experience of something new and unique and not a silly delight in novelty. And, just as Mallarmé was unable to see his Book through to the end, Segalen did not complete this basic work, though its main points were fortunately preserved. The theory of the poem is resistant to expression.

In Asia, another land of conjunction and permanence, alongside the building crises, these three poets (among others)—Segalen, Claudel, and Saint-John Perse—either met or succeeded one another. An important part of their work is played out there. But Saint-John Perse and Segalen took the road in opposite directions. Saint-John Perse began by fixing in memory, in what would be *Éloges,* the scenery of his native island, Guadeloupe. However, his real vocation was getting away, no matter how it made him suffer. Segalen, on the other hand, went toward the other, ran to elsewhere. Saint-John Perse, born in this elsewhere, returned to the Same—toward the Center. He proclaimed the universality of the French language and declared this language his country. The poems that followed attempted, to the very end, to erect the murmuring cathedrals of this chosen universal.*

Similarly, in Georges Schéhadé's poetry: the quarrying of place, the fantastic fantasy that unleashes all known geography, prophetically give an account—many years before the event—of the dramatic breakup of Lebanon, the place of Relation. Expressed there again, in the ethereal suspension

---

*The rooted errantry of this poet is discussed elsewhere.

of language, is a renunciation of the earth: a disorientation of words—which end up joining with the only available authority, the poetic grace of the French language.

This sort of effort, in which pathos contributes to genius, had its forerunners in far less convincing attempts to return and, frankly, be reintegrated through the language: the Parnassians, Leconte de Lisle, and José Maria de Heredia are examples. Without counting the immeasurable adventure, entirely on the level of the absolute, of another poet from elsewhere, who, like Saint-John Perse, wanted to "inhabit his name," making language his country: Lautréamont.

This thought of the Same and the Other[2] thus put poets at risk but became hopelessly banal as soon as emerging populations made its formulation obsolete. Converging histories have also joined forces with this contingent of the world's literatures, bringing to life new forms of expression "within" the same language. Poets from the Caribbean, the Maghreb, and other parts of Africa are not moving toward that elsewhere that is the aim of projectile movement, nor are they returning toward a Center. They create their works in metropolitan regions, where their peoples have made a sudden appearance. The old expansive trajectory and the spirituality of the itinerary (always from Paris to Jerusalem or elsewhere) yield to the world's realized compactness. We have to enter into the equivalencies of Relation.

My excuse for accumulating so many commonplaces about these tendencies so readily discernible in literature written in French is that amassing commonplaces is, perhaps, the right approach to my real subject—the entanglements of worldwide relation—and that almost everything that has been said about these tendencies, concerning the poetics of Relation, has been done so in a manner that is fragmentary, reticent, and stubbornly blind.

Because, as I have already emphasized, these trajectories (from the European here to elsewhere) end up abolishing what yesterday originally occasioned their being: the linear projection of a sensibility toward the world's horizons, the vectorization of this world into metropolises and colonies. Theoretician thought is loath to sanction this abolition— thereby shutting down its bastions. It tries to be clever with the thrust of the world and sidesteps it. It thinks up screens for itself.

In addition, the poetics of Relation remains forever conjectural and presupposes no ideological stability. It is against the comfortable assurances linked to the supposed excellence of a language. A poetics that is latent, open, multilingual in intention, directly in contact with everything possible. Theoretician thought, focused on the basic and fundamental, and allying these with what is true, shies away from these uncertain paths.

Poetry's circulation and its action no longer conjecture a given people but the evolution of the planet Earth. That too is a commonplace, one worth repeating. We have to know that this activity pinpointed here in French literatures operates for all the others, each time on the basis of a different perspective. Every expression of the humanities opens onto the fluctuating complexity of the world. Here poetic thought safeguards the particular, since only the totality of truly secure particulars guarantees the energy of Diversity. But in every instance this particular sets about Relation in a completely intransitive manner, relating, that is, with the finally realized totality of all possible particulars.

When we say that, henceforth, this poetics of Relation interweaves and no longer projects, that it inscribes itself in a circularity, we are not referring to a circuit, a line of energy curved back onto itself. Trajectory, even bent or inflected, no longer applies. How many different problematics, secreted in how many other regions of the world, and under how many different auspices, have come to encounter the problematic we raise here, organizing the rounds of the Earth totality? And then, in a circularity with volume, we imagine the discloseable aesthetics of a Chaos, with every least detail as complex as the whole that cannot be reduced, simplified, or normalized. Each of its parts patterns activity implicated in the activity of every other. The history of peoples has led to this dynamic. They need not stop running on their own momentum to join in this movement, since they are inscribed in it already. They cannot, however, "give-on-and-with" until they reach the point at which they go beyond assenting to their linear drive alone and consent to global dynamics—practicing a self-break and a reconnection.

We no longer reveal totality within ourselves by lightning flashes. We approach it through the accumulation of sediments. The poetics of duration (another leitmotiv), one of the first principles of the sacred, founding books of community, reappears to take up the relay from the poetics of the moment. Lightning flashes are the shivers of one who desires or dreams of a totality that is impossible or yet to come; duration urges on those who attempt to live this totality, when dawn shows through the linked histories of peoples.

Sediment then begins first with the country in which your drama takes shape. Just as Relation is not a pure abstraction to replace the old concept of the universal, it also neither implies nor authorizes any ecumenical detachment. The landscape of your word is the world's landscape. But its frontier is open.

The Caribbean, as far as I am concerned, may be held up as one of the places in the world where Relation presents itself most visibly, one of the explosive regions where it seems to be gathering strength.

This has always been a place of encounter and connivance and, at the same time, a passageway toward the American continent. Compared to the Mediterranean, which is an inner sea surrounded by lands, a sea that concentrates (in Greek, Hebrew, and Latin antiquity and later in the emergence of Islam, imposing the thought of the One), the Caribbean is, in contrast, a sea that explodes the scattered lands into an arc. A sea that diffracts. Without necessarily inferring any advantage whatsoever to their situation, the reality of archipelagos in the Caribbean or the Pacific provides a natural illustration of the thought of Relation. What took place in the Caribbean, which could be summed up in the word *creolization*, approximates the idea of Relation for us as nearly as possible. It is not merely an encounter, a shock (in Segalen's sense), a *métissage*,[3] but a new and original dimension allowing each person to be there and elsewhere, rooted and open, lost in the mountains and free beneath the sea, in harmony and in errantry.

If we posit *métissage* as, generally speaking, the meeting and synthesis of two differences, creolization seems to be a limitless *métissage*, its elements diffracted and its consequences unforeseeable. Creolization diffracts, whereas certain forms of *métissage* can concentrate one more time. Here it is devoted to what has burst forth from lands that are no longer islands. Its most obvious symbol is in the Creole language, whose genius consists in always being open, that is, perhaps, never becoming fixed except according to systems of variables that we have to imagine as much as define. Creolization carries along then into the adventure of multilingualism and into the incredible explosion of cultures. But the explosion of cultures does not mean they are scattered or mutually diluted. It is the violent sign of their consentual, not imposed, sharing.[4]

The same holds true, in many different ways, throughout the Americas. I cannot help thinking that these itineraries I have described for literature written in French have long been traveled by the literature of the United States in its links with its common rootstock, the English language. From the periphery to the Center with Henry James; in a total poetics of Relation with Walt Whitman; in the affirmation of differences with black American poets; in the structuring of supposed periphery as the Center, from the particular to a nongeneralizing universal, with William Faulkner ("failed poet"), whose work practically never went beyond the limits of that "postage stamp" of Yoknapatawpha County, the literary double of Oxford, Mississippi, where he chose to live.

And at stake once again in Brazilian and Hispano-American literatures: the explosion of baroque expression, the whorls of time, the mingling of centuries and jungles, the same epic voice retying into the weft of the world, beyond any imposed solitude, exaction, or oppression.

Thus what —for Segalen and so many others—was the wish of the poet discovering the world is now, for everyone, the work of the poet sharing in the life of the world.

Throughout this book I return again and again to what I have so long considered the main themes of such a poetics: the dialectics between the oral and the written, the thought of multilingualism, the balance between the present moment and duration, the questioning of literary genres, the power of the baroque, the nonprojectile imaginary construct.[5] But even this constant repetition is sufficient evidence that such a poetics never culminates in some qualitative absolute. For, in reality, Relation is not an absolute toward which every work would strive but a totality—even if for us this means disentangling it, something it never required—that through its poetic and practical and unceasing force attempts to be perfected, to be spoken, simply, that is, to be complete.

# A Rooted Errantry

For Saint-John Perse universality is optative. Not that it was predicated by him in a desolate mood (like someone who takes refuge in the thought of the universal, because he considers no specific situation his responsibility), but because, steadfastly and without pause, he projects it before himself. Saint-John Perse, indeed, left the spot toward which so many French poets who were his contemporaries projected themselves—the elsewhere full of diversity—which somehow always ends up contributing to the glorification of a sovereign Here.

The Here for him: "my bitch of Europe, who was white and poet more than I." Understand that it was not where he uttered his first cry (Guadeloupe) that Saint-John Perse engendered his poetics but in the places of its distant origins, its ideal provenance. Poetry has its source in an idea, in a desire, not in the literal fact of birth.

His elsewhere, by contrast: an island, above all a conjectural place, where apparently even the poet's birth already marked a margin. His elsewhere was not like Segalen's, colored by a dream to be approached, a temptation to be satisfied. It was given in childhood, already the evidence of every possible elsewhere.

To consecrate the union between elsewhere and possibility, the poet demanded of himself permanent abstinence from something impossible for him: the house of his birth in the Antilles but also, and as if attributable to this first abstinence, he kept a resolute distance from any Here conferred in advance (not willfully meditated).

Saint-John Perse's stern errantry sets its course wagering on a Here (Europe) toward which one must choose to return and an elsewhere (the Antilles) from which one leaves. He could not have tolerated playing colonial in the universe, as I long thought he had, nor being its vagabond, as Rimbaud attempted. He heightens the universal within himself, forging it from things impossible. These are the very reasons his universality has nothing to do with exoticism, severely criticizing it, instead, and serving as its natural negation.

The poetics thus set in play must be addressed. On a crude and elementary level of analysis one might emphasize its contradiction: Saint-John Perse, descendant of the class of colonial landholders, liked to think of himself as a Frenchman of noble stock; nurtured by the orality of Creole, he made the choice to establish himself in the purest of French styles. One could push this further, imagining the wounds there beneath the formal, lacquered surface, a drama that both cancels out and elevates itself into arrogant rigidity. But let's not. The lesson of the poet goes much deeper. It leaves behind the ordinary regions laid out in biography.

Saint-John Perse renounces any sort of "grasp" of the history of the place he was born and projects, into an eternally given future, the All he takes for his grounding. The commonplace of such a future is the name, his name as poet, one deliberately forged: a word. "I shall inhabit my name."

With these words he announces not the obsolescence of narrative but a new and original aesthetic form: the narration of the universe. This is why his writing takes on added strength from his considerable efforts as an entomologist, cartographer, or lexicographer. The rigors of material and his encyclopedic knowledge weave a controlled proliferation through which the universe overflows and recounts itself for us.

\*

Clearly, one of the places engraved in Antillean memory is the circle drawn around the storyteller by the shadows of night. On the borders of this ring the children who will relay the word are beside themselves. Their bodies are hot with the fever of day; their eyes grow larger in this time that does not go by. These children understand nothing of the formulas, nor do they catch the allusions, but the man with the stories speaks to them first. He is quick to guess when they will shiver, wide mouthed in terror, or laugh to cover up their fear. His voice comes from beyond the seas, charged with the movement of those African countries present in their absence; it lingers in the night, which draws the trembling children into its womb.

It astonishes me to hear people sometimes try to reduce Saint-John Perse's orality to that of declamation. Yet it could never be produced onstage. Too many broad zones of obviousness stretch out within it, blocked here and there by root stumps, when language thickens into nodules. When the obvious is declaimed, it immediately becomes a tautological transparency. Believing that this poet's text can fill or define the stage of a theater is a mistake too often made. His sort of orality does not lead to things of a public nature; it is the equivalent of (alternative to) modesty. Underneath, the inner voice weaves its redundant repetitions. This is an orality that is not spoken aloud but articulated in underground understandings.

The lack of any circle summing up the night around him is the first distinction between Saint-John Perse and the Antillean storyteller. There are no torches surrounding his words; there is only a hand stretched toward the horizon that rises up as ocean swells or high plateaus. It is the always possible infinite. The ring made by the voice is diffracted into the world. The orality of Saint-John Perse is not wrapped by rustling shadows suggestive of the surroundings; it greets dawns, when faraway echoes are already mingling with familiar sounds, when the caravan makes its departure from the undying desert.

Saint-John Perse does not piece back together the torn memory of one place, where another lost place still lies concealed or is finally revealed. The Antillean story, diverting the traces it maintains of an original Africa, laces the swells of this previous country into echoes and, refusing the inertia of transparent words, makes us think of the real world, this world he writes about. But this poet, likewise, who begins by "celebrating a childhood," refuses the comforts of an album to be leafed through. What, in fact, is this always vanishing memory? What is this place (this house) the one they say we come from? And this princely solitude in the midst of "all things" dazzling, exploded, and permanently bright? The work of Saint-John Perse aims at pushing memory (of a place, of people, of the things seen in childhood) far forward. This orality does not invite listeners to the shadow's edge; it throws each one of us into the resolution of one to come. *Éloges* is not a tormented memory that is repeated in shadows but the suspense heralding solemn departures. The poet knows that he has absolutely lost the thing he always remembers, the thing he leaves behind.

In the works of Saint-John Perse there exist simultaneously a totalization one might call baroque and a revolution in the technique of the plainsong. They work together. But I am confident that this is a "naturalized" baroque; that is, it has nothing to do with any reference and would be opposed to it. Rerouting [*détournement*] is its only norm, or its fundamental nature. And plainsong here, ordinarily an occasion for transport or escape, holds us clearly in the world at its fullest.

Thus, it is around interactions of memory and place that things irreconcilable for both poet and storyteller are perpetrated. The Antillean locus appears to Saint-John Perse with a dazzling clarity that I would mistrust. Isn't the memory for detail (this poetics of diffracted moments) employed here in order to ward off something else: the temptation of something stirring for so long in the background of the Caribbean landscape? It is at this moment in the work that the explosion of the instant obliterates duration, which will later be recovered but under the auspices of universality. In contrast, in the orality of the Antillean story the drive of this duration (of this collective memory—of this "history"—whose energy must be made wholeheartedly clear) cancels out the detail of the place. Obsession with a possible duration clouds the explosive dazzle of the present.

For Saint-John Perse, however, as for the man who tells the tales, the same avenue awaits. In the poem's harsh transcendence, as in the cunning organization of the story, there are ruptures and densities of orality that call up these impossible things: for the latter the place where he remains and for the former the world where he goes.

Dweller and pilgrim live this same exile.

\*

Departure and errantry in Saint-John Perse are to be interpreted as a rejection of the histories of peoples but their magnificence as an assuming of History, in the Hegelian sense. This errantry is not rhizomatic but deeply rooted: in a will and an Idea. History or its negation, the intuition of the One, these are the magnetic poles of Western thought at which Saint-John Perse grounded his name. He thought that the condition of freedom is that the individual not be ruled by a history, except one that generalizes, nor limited by a place, unless that place is spiritual. Because the universal has this heroic dimension, we are able to recognize ourselves in his work, even though we challenge its generalizing models.

It may also be possible that this passion driving the work (because it is foreign to a space and a time—the Antillean history and place—that are so problematic for it and because it is rooted in such absolute errantry) is reassuring to us regarding the contradictions we experience here and now.

For the poetry of Saint-John Perse, though it is not the epic linking together of lessons from a past, augurs a new mode of connection with the Other, which, paradoxically,

41

and precisely because of this passion for errantry, prophesies the poetics of Relation. By constantly moving on, one can gather stones and weave the materiality of the universe from which Saint-John Perse created his narrative. This is how, in the end, he met with Victor Segalen, about whom he said little, doubtless because in the same sumptuous manner, but in opposite directions, their itineraries parted.

*

Unaware of us, he precedes us on this road through the world. When we catch up with him, we find him still and always drawing for us figures of our solitudes to share—though these are figures frozen in his noble renunciation.

II

# ELEMENTS

*The elementary reconstitutes itself absolutely*

# REPETITIONS

*This flood of convergences, publishing itself in the guise of the commonplace. No longer is the latter an accepted generality, suitable and dull—no longer is it deceptively obvious, exploiting common sense—it is, rather, all that is relentlessly and endlessly reiterated by these encounters. On every side the idea is being relayed. When you awaken an observation, a certainty, a hope, they are already struggling somewhere, elsewhere, in another form.*

*Repetition, moreover, is an acknowledged form of consciousness both here and elsewhere. Relentlessly resuming something you have already said. Consenting to an infinitesimal momentum, an addition perhaps unnoticed that stubbornly persists in your knowledge.*

*The difficulty: to keep this growing pile of common places from ending up as dispirited grumbling—may art provide! The probability: that you come to the bottom of all confluences to mark more strongly your inspirations.*

# Expanse and Filiation

In the Western world the hidden cause (the consequence) of both Myth and Epic is filiation, its work setting out upon the fixed linearity of time, always toward a projection, a project. We can guess that energy circulated by philosophies of the One in the West reinvigorated these imperatives of filiation. Wherever time was not conceived of as linear—India, for example—or where philosophers contemplated not the One but the All, the founding myths did not generate the process of filiation.* Conceptions of the origins of the world (its creation) were not corroborated in a genealogical sequence that would have rooted the species (race or people) in this first act.

The retelling (certifying) of a "creation of the world" in a filiation guarantees that this same filiation—or legitimacy—rigorously ensues simply by describing in reverse the trajectory of the community, from its present to this act of creation. This view is not at the origin of every Western myth, but it is the view that prevailed, determining the evolution of these cultures.

In every instance, and of necessity, the mythical community precedes any thought of the individual, whose foremost dimension is as a link in the chain of filiation.

*Among the Mayan and Aztec peoples a cyclical time—buttressed by a passion for dating events—coincided with a tendency toward filiation, reaching back as far as possible through ancient times, without, however, anchoring itself in an undoubtable "creation" of the world.

Buddhist mythologies, to offer an almost commonplace comparison, are based on temporal cycles and consider first of all, and uniquely, the individual (himself impermanent or almost so), whose "stories" are of self-perfection through dissolution into the All. The Buddha is the exemplary, but not necessarily original, individuation, whose oneness is due to this fulfillment. The One is distinguished from oneness, by the total lack of any generalizable understanding in this latter. Aided by a collection of ritual precepts that do not constitute a body of Knowledge, each individual will strive to follow from afar the example of Buddha. The community's chronology—its linearity (which in the West becomes History)—is completely ineffectual there.*

Western mythologies, in contrast, conceive of the individual only insofar as he is a participant in the community. It took the appearance of Christ (who broke away from Hebrew community participation, though relying on it, and brought humanity into Christian universality) for the individual as such to sublimate in his dignity the evolution of the community.

The chain of filiation (as hidden cause) would not, however, be despised or rejected at that point. Christ is above all the Son. He consecrates filiation: being a descendant of David and at the same time the Son of God who is God—and, perhaps, of whom it would be heresy to say that *he too* is God.

Christian individuation did not result in a return flow of history, a cyclical renewal; on the contrary, by universalizing linear time—*before and after Christ*—it brought a chronology of the human race into general use, initiating a History of Humanity. It has been suggested that, in this instance, Christ

*I qualify this assessment as far as Chinese cultures are concerned. At least to my knowledge (mediocre at best) we have not yet, perhaps, been able to study the full-sense these cultures attribute to historical relation or whether or not they envisage philosophies of History.

(We are recapitulating what we know of these movements, in an attempt to consider how they have come into our view. And frequently we make mistakes. What is important is that we start retracing the path for ourselves.)

48

marked a decisive break, uniting the histories of communities into this generalized History.

This chain of Christian filiation, however, would no longer be considered absolute at the moment that another continuous sequence, this time based on science, inscribed the human race within the network of evolution. In the end this network is only an objectivized vision of the old filiation, applied not to the legitimacy of an ethnic community but to the natural universality of all known species.

At that moment the generalization inspired by Christ was picked up by Darwin's generalizing theory, though initially they opposed each other. Both were concerned with transcending the old mythical filiation linked to the destiny of a community, to go beyond this with a universalizing notion that would retain, however, the power of the principle of linearity and that "grasped" and justified History.

Paradoxically, in Buddhist thought, in which the aim is to dissolve the individual within the All, there is only individuation. In Western systems of thought, solicitous of the dignity of the human individual and originating with individual adventure, there ends up being—another paradox—only generalization. Philosophies based on the One bear within them the embryo of History (whether Natural History or the History of Humanity).

As Mediterranean myths tell us, thinking about One is not thinking about All. These myths express communities, each one innocently transparent for self and threateningly opaque for the other. They are functional, even if they take obscure or devious means. They suggest that the self's opacity for the other is insurmountable, and, consequently, no matter how opaque the other is for oneself (no myth ever provides for the legitimacy of the other), it will always be a question of reducing this other to the transparency experienced by oneself. Either the other is assimilated, or else it is annihilated. That is the whole principle of generalization and its entire process.

Myth, therefore, contains a hidden violence that catches in the links of filiation and absolutely challenges the existence of the other as an element of relation. The same is true of the Epic, which singles out a community in relation to the Other, and senses Being only as in-itself, because it never conceives of it as relation.

Whether in myth or epic, not only does Being (I would call it Being-as-Being) obviously not partake of the nature of the individual, but there is not even a "premonition" of individuality in the epic. Then, with Plato, the individual becomes the tomb of the soul. In this way the philosopher introduces the process of individuation and generalization into the tradition of Near Eastern thought, where it is sometimes harmonious, sometimes conflicting. This will be completed (resolved) in the occurrence of Christ. Christ, and He alone, manifested incarnation without the Fall, filiation without the weight of heredity. In him Parmenidean Being and Platonic soul are joined. It is, however, possible to make a case for the real "break" in Western thought having taken place with Plato.

Filiation is explicit in the Old Testament; it is implicit in the *Iliad,* in which the reputed or chosen sons of Gods play out the projected rivalries of the Immortals among themselves. It is legitimacy that is disrupted by the abduction of Helen (with its threat of *métissage*—mixing the blood of East and West); and legitimacy, perhaps, inseparable from the project of discovery and knowledge, provides the tragic driving force for the *Odyssey* (Ulysses and Penelope's faithfulness to each other); legitimacy, in any case (with the realization of *métissage*), is the cause of weakness in the epic of Alexander. Filiation is indispensable for the *Aeneid.* And, if Dante does not have recourse to it in *The Divine Comedy* (because Christ had already realized the universal Church by then), he nonetheless places his journey into hell—in short, into our world—under the enlightened guidance of Virgil (tu duca, tu segnore, e tu maestro). He does so not simply because Virgil was at that time the master of poetics but also because he went beyond the break at the time of Christ to reestablish continuity (through concern with filiation and its action) with one of the matrices of Myth, the city of Troy. From Homer to Virgil the threat of *métissage* ceased to seem calamitous. Thus, from the outset *The Divine Comedy*, one of the greatest monuments of Christian universalization, stresses the filiation shared by the ancient myths and the new religion linking both to the creation of the world.

If I try to simplify, reducing and summarizing my thoughts concerning these two Western "movements" of generalization (Christian and Darwinian), and if I compare them with things I think I know about their Buddhist equivalent, I come up with the following formulation:

CHRIST.— To an undivided ethnic community, with the legitimacy of filiation, an individualizing act that inaugurates a History of Humanity is appended. Thus, the exclusive linearity of this filiation is succeeded by the undiversifiable linearity of a generalization.

DARWIN.— To an original indistinction the process of Selection that governs evolution and determines the distinction among genera and species is applied. The linearity of the process leads into the diversifiable generalization of Natural History.

BUDDHA.— Through a primordial movement of circularity the individual strives in search of perfection toward a dissolution within the All. His successive lives are the cycles ("the histories") of this perfection and do not constitute a linearity. At the end of a process he is reincarnated: he is the same and yet other.

It is scarcely important that Christian generalization originated in a choice, whereas Darwinian generalization was the result of an objective observation. Both are linked to an identical spirit of universality—in opposition to community's exclusivity or to Nature's heterogeneity; both reach fulfillment at the end of a line; both already are and further become the propagation of a Knowledge. The Buddhist gyre never proceeds from generalization: it is not linear and does not depart from individualization. The approach to Nirvana is impossible to generalize through knowledge but is particularized through knowledges.

The consequence (the hidden cause) of both Epic and Tragedy, then, is legitimacy.

Tragedy springs from any situation in which community consent is threatened. Something is "tragic" because the threat will not be discovered (held off or deferred) until the moment in which the community *feels* that the chain of filiation has been broken. The tragic action is the uncovering of what had gone unnoticed.

Engendering tragedy, it is illegitimacy that threatens the community by leading toward its dissolution. Tragic action, the art of opacity and disclosure, resolves this dissolution in the quest for legitimacy and its reestablishment. This same quest, in myth and epic, guaranteed the strict succession through which every community linked itself to the first act of Creation. If legitimacy is ruptured, the chain of filiation is no longer meaningful, and the community wanders the world, no longer able to lay claim to any primordial necessity. Tragic action absorbs this unbalance.

Tragic action is progressive and carried out within opacity, because the violence linked to filiation (the absolute exclusion of the other) cannot be faced head on nor all at once. Such a confrontation would have left the community reeling from a surfeit of understanding, a sort of short-circuit of consciousness. Wars and conquests mask for the community the violence of this exclusion of the other. But things that one can valiantly endure in battle, whose pretext has been calculated or improvised, become unbearable in the sacred contemplation of the root. Whence the importance in tragedy of the art of unveiling. Oedipus would be incapable of conceiving "at first sight" the truth that lies within him.

This is also why the City is threatened by the same force

that elects within it a para-fate hero, focusing the thunderbolt, who takes it upon himself to resolve the dissolution. Public consciousness was incapable of discussing a resolution: generalizing (politicizing) the discussion would have meant the community was no longer inscribed in the primordial and sacred legitimacy provided by filiation but in the problematic (threatening) relation to the other. This relation would already consist of what, without elaborating, I call "expanse" [*l'étendue*].

This explains why the attempts—in Greek theater—to shore up (to "expand") the power of tragedy (by diversifying and multiplying characters, exposing their motives—all those "improvements" from Aeschylus to Sophocles to Euripides) serve equally as paths leading away from sacred awe, until gradually theater's citizen forms—drama, comedy, etc.—are introduced.

In an exemplary case, that of Oedipus, Freudian reinterpretation of the myth confirms the process of filiation implicated there and attempts to generalize this process. But we shall see that what opposes this new sort of generalization is, in fact, the expansion, power, and reality that we shall define, whose presupposition is the opposite of filiation.

Shakespeare is considered to have confirmed this work of legitimacy in his theater. If there is something rotten in Denmark, it is because the "line" of succession to the throne has been broken, demanding catharsis with Hamlet as victim. During this same period Camoens, in his epic poetry, was renouncing the sacrifice of a propitiating hero, singing instead of a community of heroes who set off to conquer the world.

In *The Tempest*, however, Shakespeare conceived of these two dimensions, both founding legitimacy and power of conquest, as ultimately working together. It is because Prospero is the legitimate duke of Milan that he has authority over Caliban, the elements, and the universe. Here the destiny of the City expands according to the dimensions of the known and colonizable world. It is not, in the end, through the sacrifice (or punishment) of the hero that things in dissolution are resolved but through the reestablishment of his power, formerly usurped. Prospero is distinguished, in fact, from Hamlet, Macbeth, Richard III, and the whole stream of claimants to the English throne (all characters thrust into situations that "will turn out well": through their sacrifice or their extermination, that is, through a return to legitimacy), precisely for that reason: he is the beneficiary, right from the start, of this legitimacy. For this same reason *The Tempest* is not a tragedy but a heroic/historical drama. Because, if the play "turns out well," it is not from the point of view of the community (the city of Milan, which had never been threatened by dissolution—the usurper, Prospero's brother, moreover, never having seemed particularly serious). It is solely from the point of view of the hero, the bearer of Westernness, in order to assert the legitimacy of his power over the world. A decolonized Caliban occupies this expanse and challenges Prospero's projective legitimacy. He does so in two ways, the same two that from the beginnings of time have made it possible to relay mythic, epic, or tragic obscurity: through the individual ardor of lyricism and the collective practice of politics.

When, in fact, epic and tragedy had run their course in the West (after the City had reassured itself about its own existence), they yielded to these two modes: the lyric and the political, both out in the open, where individuals were engaged as human persons, that is, as individuals apart from the sacred mystery of the collective community.

Yet the lyrics and politics of Caliban revived this mystery, with all its epic power and tragic disclosure, and did so, moreover, without returning to the intolerance underlaid by Myth, thus opening out onto a new order of community (of the planet Earth, henceforth so fragile and threatened) whose legitimacy is still neither self-evident nor sanctioned. Tragedy has here a new requirement, a new object for its renewed art of disclosure.

Today it is not only the legitimacy of cultures that is threatened in the world (the life energy of peoples); also threatened are their relations of equivalency. A modern epic and a modern tragedy would offer to unite the specificity of nations, granting each culture's opacity (though no longer as *en-soi*) yet at the same time imagining the transparency of their relations. Imagining. Because this transparency is precisely not *en-soi*. It is not rooted in any specific legitimacy, which thus implies that the disclosure of tragedy would be directed toward a continuum (in expansion) and not toward a past (set in filiation).

Modern epic and modern tragedy would express political consciousness (no longer an impossible naive consciousness) but one disengaged from civic frenzy; they would ground lyricism in a confluence of speech and writing. In this confluence things of the community, without being diminished (and without turning truths into generalities as Christian tragedy—in the work of Eliot or Claudel—meant to do), would be the initiation to totality without renouncing the particular. In that way modern epic and modern tragedy would make the specific relative, without having to merge the Other (the expanse of the world) into a reductive transparency.*

Reticulated in such a network, the former sacred power of filiation would not be the exclusive player; the resolution of elements in dissolution here would be relayed by the aggregation of things that are scattered. This is what Segalen called the action of Diversity. No longer would the sacrifice of a propitiating, or victim-hero be required; for we are able to untangle this web, pondering it together and recognizing ourselves side by side within it.

We will look straight at the sacred, the assumed order in the disorder of Relation, without being stricken with awe. We will discuss it without the solemn chant of the Greek Chorus

*The imagined transparency of Relation is, in that way, the opposite of the reductive transparency of the generalizing universal.

for our sole influence. We will imagine it without divining the hand of a god there full force. To imagine the tranparency of Relation is also to justify the opacity of what impels it. The sacred is of us, of this network, of our wandering, our errantry.

There (here) the idea of filiation, its energy, its linear force, no longer function—for us; nor is the root setting and conquering legitimacy an imperative; nor, consequently, is any ontologically based generalization required.

At the moment that the West projected into the world for the first time, this began to be realized. This project of discovery and ascendancy was taken to be an absolute value. It was even asserted that both geographical discoveries and the conquests of science were driven by the same audacity and the same capacity for generalization. Territorial conquest and scientific discovery (the terms are interchangeable) were reputed to have equal worth. The absolute of ancient filiation and conquering linearity, the project of knowledge and arrowlike nomadism, each used the other in its growth. But I maintain that, right from the first shock of conquest, this movement contained the embryo (no matter how deferred its realization might have seemed) that would transcend the duality that started it.

Let us, then, press on past this duality. Let us not start by confusing discovery and conquest, which was the point of Daniel Boorstin's book about scientific disclosure, *The Discoverers* (whose subtitle in the French translation by Robert Laffone [1989] is "From Herodotus to Copernicus—From Christopher Columbus to Einstein—The adventures of the men who invented the world"). Which means, of course, that these masters of the Voyage and these masters of Knowledge are one and the same. At the end of chapter 26, "An Empire without Wants," Boorstin writes: "Fully equipped with the technology, the intelligence, and the national resources to become discoverers, the Chinese doomed themselves to be the discovered."[1]

A judgment of this sort implies that, in Relation, the ones

who "discovered" retain absolutely the advantages of this action. But Relation does not "grasp" any such antecedent. The terra incognita lying before us is an inexhaustible sphere of variations born of the contact among cultures. Disclosure applies to this inexhaustibility in an expansion of a different sort. "Discovery," projection, arrowlike nomadism, or project of knowledge, becomes lost there or gains through the network. The powers of domination prosper there, but legitimacies are dead.*

William Faulkner's *Absalom! Absalom!* following lessons learned from the Oedipus myth (or, later, the Oedipus complex), concerns a possible incest, a perversion of filiation. But the decisive—fatal—element would be part of another "causal series": that is, the intrusion of Negro blood. At first, in the planter Sutpen's first wife, a Haitian woman, it was undiscernible. Once this black stock was discovered (recalling how southern aristocratic families in the United States usually dread and are frequently haunted by this sort of "misdeed" committed by careless great-grandparents), Sutpen, the founder, decided to repudiate mother and son and to replant his stock in Mississippi. But neither founding nor filiation can be begun again, and Sutpen's history catches up with him. That this first son whom he had cast out into the void and the daughter of his second marriage would come to love each other is calamity enough; but the discovery that his first son, despite his appearance, is Negro (which Sutpen alone had known for a long time) finally brings together the conditions for filiation to dissolve permanently into the new expanse of extension. This is the double object of disclosure in the novel. Incest changes the course of filiation, and vice versa; for the novel suggests that there (in the South) incest

*Ideological thought is not going to be satisfied with the expression "powers of domination" but will demand that the terms—political, economic, or cultural— be specified. But we know today that these terms cannot be calculated a priori and that each time, in each locus of domination, through the resistance of those oppressed, a precise and not generalizable sense of the oppression here and now emerges.

might be accepted, conceived of, but not the intrusion of black blood—which is nonetheless there.

Expanse: in which Africa (for us a source and a mirage, retained in a simplified representation) has, therefore, its role to play. In all of Faulkner's work the pileup of patronyms, of mixings of blood whether forced or not, of double lineages (black and white), relentlessly reproduces and almost caricatures the extended family style that has so long contributed to the formation of the Caribbean social fabric. It is no accident that Sutpen, unknowingly at first, encountered his fate in Haiti. The protagonists of this story, except for the ones chosen by their innocence—epic being naive—to be its narrators, are stricken by a tragic stupor (a word so similar in my mind to Sutpen that I pronounced it Stutpen for a long time). But the tragic crisis, magnificently and ritually brought to completion in the burning of the House of Sutpen, will not restore legitimacy; on the contrary, this moment consecrates the inevitable obliteration of it. Faulknerian tragedy is at odds with that of Aeschylus: it does not contribute to reestablishing the balance of a community; it commits the heresy of destroying the sacredness of filiation; it closes the history of the sons of Solomon forever and lays out the prospect open to the sons of Snopes, the unmitigated upstart. Like any great tragic system, Faulkner's work ignores, that is, it encompasses and goes beyond, politics and lyricism, but it makes us contend with their contemporary poles: violence and opacity.

(Expanse [extending] ramifies its web. Leap and variance, in another poetics. Transversality. Quantifiable infinity. Unrealized quantity. Inexhaustible tangle. Expanse [extending] is not merely space; it is also its own dreamed time.)

(Let's open another and deciding parenthesis: the Oedipus complex does not function in the expanse that is extension. Neither mothering nor fathering are factors there. The Oedipus complex depends on laws of filiation, whereas an extended family is circular and meshed, as is the web of Faulkner's work. (And within this parenthesis we'll open yet another: that all the interpretations (of our societies) dominated by themes of filiation—the phallic, the oedipal, the maternal complex, etc., and you must admit there are more of these than there is need for them—epitomize ethnocentric and frequently naive projections of Western thought. If we take this further: in Roger Dragonetti's *La vie de la lettre au Moyen Age* (Paris: Editions du Seuil, 1980) I picked up an interesting observation concerning the feminine character of the (maternal) languages that appeared in the Middle Ages, as opposed to the normative, paternal authority of Latin:

> The privilege accorded to the femininity of language (the reverse image of the theology of the Father) arises with the birth of romance languages. The result of this is that in preference to Latin the mystery of the poetry of languages is conclusively joined with the mystery of *mother tongues,* languages of the desire whose distant essence, the indeterminate and indeterminable object of every quest, is symbolized in turns by the *fin'amor,* the sister, the lady, the queen or the virgin-mother. (45–46)

A valuable observation, yet one that I think would not apply in the context of our Caribbean cultures, for example, in the emergence of the Creole language. The French language during the period of creolization was not the sole language of literacy, as Latin was during the Middle Ages (even if there did exist from the eighth to the eleventh centuries a *lingua romana rustica*). It was, instead, a living idiom that was playing out its history elsewhere—there (here) where, even more important, all imposition of filiation had been forsaken. The legitimacy confirming filiation in patriarchal societies also implies femininity as the locus of a counterforce, generally of a spiritual order. This is what Dragonetti found happening at the birth of romance languages. In matriarchal societies legitimacy was "natural" (impossible, for example, to doubt the function of the mother) and could not have been raised to the status of a value.* African cultures, consequently, despite the "chain" of Ancestors, do not seem to me to obey filiation's hidden violence. The same is true of our heterogeneous societies. Creole tongues, mother tongues vary too much within them to "be conjoined," to be prized as an essence or to be valorized as a symbol of either the mother or the father. Their threatened violence is, admittedly, a synthesis but one spread throughout the expanse. This violence has been brought to a crisis by a new fact that is suddenly part of the existence of contemporary languages: their widespread and uneasy consciousness that they are subject to disappearance. Languages no longer die away gently; they no longer develop innocently. No symbolic system can resist all this stuff). Just as early discoverers/discovered are equal in Relation, the legitimate and its opposite appeal to each other. That is, legitimacy is totally replaced by contingency. (Someone has suggested to me that *adoption* has a truly generative function.) I am fully aware of the forms of domination perpetuated by present-day heirs of the discoverers and of their intentions to restore filiation "elsewhere"—by imposing

*These analyses about background do not stop us from observing that oppression of women can intensify in the heart of a matrifocal society. (I would still hesitate to describe Antillean societies as matrilinear.) In large part the respective attitudes of men and women in their relations here were determined by colonial pressures. Collective dependence reinforced the "reproductive" machismo of male slaves but did not authorize the appearance of femininity as a spiritual counterforce, even if women were frequently centers of resistance. This is why, perhaps, at least this is what I think, the women of Martinique and in many colonized countries have a tendency in their socialization to disregard feminism and to pass directly to various conquests of power, both social and political. Feminism is, also, the luxury by means of which women in the West through their struggles transform their ancient pseudopower, their spiritual counterforce into real equality. Be that as it may, there is an equally high number of equally intense violent incidents, rapes, and incest in which women are the victims everywhere.

familial or cultural models and ways of life or settings for this—wherever it had not already exerted its silent power to put down roots. But taking root, henceforth, will be of a different nature. It is in relation. Filiation cannot be replanted elsewhere; its myth is not infinitely disclosable; and Oedipus cannot be exported—into the expanse of extension).

What, then, will both violence and opacity be for us in Relation? It was to better assess such questions that we embarked on these interweaving journeys to the sources of Western thoughts—thoughts aimed at, but not inventing, the world.

Today the ancient intolerant violence of filiation is shaken up in the anarchistic violence of clashing cultures, in which no projection imposes its line and in which—this bears repeating— legitimacy (with its resultant imperative succession of the law and order of reasons, linked to the order derived from possessions and conquests) comes undone.

Inherited domination stemming from conquest and possession persists and grows more attractive, but within these voluminous circularities the lines become lost: light shed by ideological analysis is no longer enough to flush this domination into the open.* The resistance to contemporary forms of domination, too visible and at the same time undetectable and untouchable, is in turn limited in time and place, with no possibility (at the moment) of support from another locus of resistance. Internationals of suffering cannot be publicly structured in this circularity, even though Internationals of oppression are secretly planted there.

If it is true that the intolerant violence of filiation was formerly buried in the sacred mystery of the root, and that entering into the opacity of this mystery was tragically granted, and if this opacity therefore both signified the mystery and simultaneously masked its violence—this always took

*I include under the heading "ideology" critical and political philosophies that have contributed to "revealing" ideologies.

place in function of a final underlying transparency in the tragic struggle. This same transparency, in Western History, predicts that a common truth of Mankind exists and maintains that what approaches it most closely is action that projects, whereby the world is realized at the same time that it is caught in the act of its foundation.

Against this reductive transparency, a force of opacity is at work. No longer the opacity that enveloped and reactivated the mystery of filiation but another, considerate of all the threatened and delicious things joining one another (without conjoining, that is, without merging) in the expanse of Relation.

Thus, that which protects the Diverse we call opacity. And henceforth we shall call Relation's imaginary a transparency, one that for ages (ever since the Pre-Socratics? or the Mayans? in Timbuktu already? ever since the pre-Islamic poets and the Indian storytellers?) has had premonitions of its unforeseeable whirl.

For centuries "generalization," as operated by the West, brought different community tempos into an equivalency in which it attempted to give a hierarchical order to the times they flowered. Now that the panorama has been determined and equidistances described, is it not, perhaps, time to return to a no less necessary "degeneralization"? Not to a replenished outrageous excess of specificities but to a total (dreamed-of) freedom of the connections among them, cleared out of the very chaos of their confrontations.

62

# Closed Place, Open Word

1

The Plantation system spread, following the same structural principles, throughout the southern United States, the Caribbean islands, the Caribbean coast of Latin America, and the northeastern portion of Brazil. It extended throughout the countries (including those in the Indian Ocean), constituting what Patrick Chamoiseau and Raphaël Confiant call the territory of *créolité* [creoleness].[1] There are grounds for understanding why, despite very different linguistic areas engaged in very divergent political dynamics, the same organization would create a rhythm of economic production and form the basis for a style of life. That takes care of the spatial aspect.

Regarding time, or, if you will, our grasp of the histories that converged in these spaces, two other questions need to be addressed. The first concerns the system's evolution: Why was there no continuation of it anywhere—no social structure organically derived from it, with coherent or contradictory repercussions, inscribed in any enduring aspect? The Plantation system collapsed everywhere, brutally or progressively, without generating its own ways of superseding itself. The second question is even more amazing: How did a system that was so fragile give rise, paradoxically, to what are seen as the modern vectors of civilization, in the not untolerant sense that this word henceforth holds for us?

Let us sum up in a few connected phrases what we know of the Plantation. It is an organization formed in a social pyramid, confined within an enclosure, functioning apparently as an autarky but actually dependent, and with a technical mode of production that cannot evolve because it is based on a slave structure.

A pyramid organization: everywhere after 1848 the origin of the mass of slaves, then workers, was African—or Hindu in the Caribbean; the middle level, managers, administrators, and overseers, were hired men of European origin, a small number of whom were replaced early in this century by people of color—once again in the Caribbean; at the top of the pyramid were the planters, colonists, or *békés,* as they were called in the Antilles, who strove to constitute a white pseudoaristocracy. I say pseudo because almost nowhere were these attempts at putting down roots within a tradition sanctioned by the stamp of time nor by any legitimacy of absolute filiation. Plantations, despite secreting manners and customs, from which cultures ensued, never established any tradition of great impact.

An enclosed place: each Plantation was defined by boundaries whose crossing was strictly forbidden; impossible to leave without written permission or unless authorized by some ritual exception, such as Carnival time. Chapel or church, stockrooms for distributing supplies or later the grocery story, infirmary or hospital: everything was taken care of within a closed circle. Now the following is what we need to understand: How could a series of autarkies, from one end to the other of the areas involved, from Louisiana to Martinique to Réunion, be capable of kinship? If each Plantation is considered as a closed entity, what is the principle inclining them to function in a similar manner?

Finally, the reality of slavery. It was decisive, of course, in the stagnation of production techniques. An insurmountable tendency toward technical irresponsibility resulted from it, especially among slaveholders. And when technical innovations, mechanization, and industrialization occurred, as they did, for example, in the southern United States, it was already too late. Social dynamics had taken other routes than cane traces, sugarcane alleys, or avenues of magnolias. As for the slaves or their close descendants, who had absolutely no interest in the Plantation's yield, they would be an exception to this technical irresponsibility because of their own need to guarantee daily survival on the edges of the system. This resulted in the widespread development of small occupations, or what is referred to in the Antilles as *djobs,* a habitual economy of bits and scraps. Technical irresponsibility on the one hand and a breakdown into individual operations on the other: immobility and fragmentation lay at the heart of the system eating away at it.

Let us, nonetheless, consult these ruins with their uncertain evidence, their extremely fragile monuments, their frequently incomplete, obliterated, or ambiguous archives. You can guess already what we are to discover: that the Plantation is one of the focal points for the development of present-day modes of Relation. Within this universe of domination and oppression, of silent or professed dehumanization, forms of humanity stubbornly persisted. In this outmoded spot, on the margins of every dynamic, the tendencies of our modernity begin to be detectable. Our first attempt must be to locate just such contradictions.

One of these contradictions contrasts the tidy composition of such a universe—in which social hierarchy corresponds in maniacal, minute detail to a mercilessly maintained racial hierarchy—with the ambiguous complexities otherwise proceeding from it.

Airtight seals were apparently the rule of the Plantation. Not simply the tight social barrier but also an irremediable break between forms of sensibility, despite each one's effects upon the other. Saint-John Perse and Faulkner, two authors born in Plantation regions and to whom I constantly turn, not surprisingly, with my questions, provide us with a chance to assess this split. We recall the famous description, if it is a description, in *Éloges:*

> *but I shall still long remember*
> *mute faces, the colour of papaya and of boredom that*
> *paused like burnt-out stars behind our chairs . . .*[2]

That papaya and that boredom—seeing people as things—do not so much emphasize the poet's distance as they reveal the radical separation (that imposible apartheid) presiding over the life of the emotions in the Plantation. I have also noted that Faulkner, who spoke so frequently of blacks, never sets out to write one of the interior monologues, of which he is such a master, for one of these characters; whereas he dares do so for some of the mulattoes in his work and even, in a tour de force now classic, for the idiot Benjy at the beginning of his novel *The Sound and the Fury.* Thus Lucas, the black character who is the principal hero of *Intruder in the Dust,* is never interiorized by Faulkner; he is described entirely through postures and gestures, a silhouette filled in against a horizon. *Intruder in the Dust* is not a novel concerning an essence but, rather, an attempt at a phenomenological approach. In the same novel Faulkner, moreover, is explicit about his narrator's understanding—or lack thereof—of the southern black: "Because he knew Lucas Beauchamp too—as well that is as any white person knew him. Better than any maybe."[3] As if the novelist, rejected by members of his class and misunderstood by the black Americans who have had access to his work, had premonitions of an impossibility brought to a head by history. The break exerts itself here.

But the break did not form delimited territories, in which the various levels of population were sectioned off. The claim that they were reciprocally extraneous did not prevent contaminations, inevitable within the enclosure of the Plantation. Despite the insistent, cold ferocity of Father Labat's writing, for example, beneath the words of this seventeenth-century chronicler of the Antilles one can feel a curiosity, riveted, anxious, and obsessive, whenever he broaches the subject of these slaves that he struggles so hard to keep calm. Fear, fantasies, and perhaps a barely willing flicker of complicity form the undercurrent of the revolts and repressions. The long list of martyrdoms is also a long *métissage*, whether involuntary or intentional.

A second contradiction contrasts the Plantation's will to autarky with its dependence, in reality, in relation to the external world. The transactions it fostered with this world took place in the elementary form of the exchange of goods, usually at a loss. Payment was in kind, or as an equivalent exchange value, which led to accumulation neither of experience nor of capital. Nowhere did the Planters manage to set up organisms that were sufficiently solid and autonomous to allow them to have access to the control of a market, means of international transportation, an independent system of money, or an efficient and specific representation in foreign markets. The Plantations, entities turned in upon themselves, paradoxically, have all the symptoms of extroversion. They are dependent, by nature, on someplace elsewhere. In their practice of importing and exporting, the established politics is not decided from within. One could say, in fact, that, socially, the Plantation is not the product of a politics but the emanation of a fantasy.

And, if we come even closer to this enclosed place, this Locus Solus, trying to imagine what its inner ramifications may be, auscultating the memory or guts inside it, then the contradictions become madness. I shall not attempt any description here. This current year would not suffice. And we are familiar enough with the countless novels and films inspired by this universe to know already that, from north to south and from west to east, the same conditions of life repeat themselves. Rather, I shall turn to another synthesizing aspect, in this case both oral and written expression—literature—stemming either directly or indirectly from the Plantation.

2

No matter which region we contemplate from among those covered by the system, we find the same trajectory and almost the same forms of expression. We could mark out three moments: literary production—first as an act of survival, then as a dead end or a delusion, finally as an effort or passion of memory.

An act of survival. In the silent universe of the Plantation, oral expression, the only form possible for the slaves, was discontinuously organized. As tales, proverbs, sayings, songs appeared—as much in the Creole-speaking world as elsewhere—they bore the stamp of this discontinuity. The texts seem to neglect the essentials of something that Western realism, from the beginning, had been able to cover so well: the situation of landscapes, the lesson of scenery, the reading of customs, the description of the motives of characters. Almost never does one find in them any concrete relating of daily facts and deeds; what one does find, on the other hand, is a symbolic evocation of situations. As if these texts were striving for disguise beneath the symbol, working to say without saying. This is what I have referred to elsewhere as detour,[4] and this is where discontinuity struggles; the same discontinuity the Maroons created through that other detour called *marronnage*.

Here we have a form of literature striving to express something it is forbidden to refer to and finding risky retorts to this organic censorship every time. The oral literature of the Plantations is consequently akin to other subsistance—survival—techniques set in place by the slaves and their immediate descendants. Everywhere that the obligation to get around the rule of silence existed a literature was created that has no "natural" continuity, if one may put it that way, but, rather, bursts forth in snatches and fragments. The storyteller is a handyman, the *djobbeur* of the collective soul.

Though this phenomenon is widespread throughout the system, nonetheless, it is within the Creole-speaking realm that it stands out most conspicuously. That is because, in addition to this obligation to get around something, the Creole language has another, internal obligation: to renew itself in every instance on the basis of a series of forgettings. Forgetting, that is, integration, of what it starts from: the multiplicity of African languages on the one hand and European ones on the other, the nostalgia, finally, for the Caribbean remains of these.* The linguistic movement of creolization proceeded through very rapid, interrupted, successive settlings of these contributions; the synthesis resulting from this process never became fixed in its terms, despite having asserted from the beginning the durability of its structures. In other words, the Creole text is never presented linguistically as an edict or a relay, on the basis of which some literary progression might be detected, with another text coming along to perfect the former, and so on. I do not know if this diffraction (through which multilingualism is, perhaps, really at work, in an underground way, for one of the first known times in the history of humanities) is indicative of all languages in formation—here, for example, we would have to study the European Middle Ages—or if it is entirely attribut-

*It is the problem of "forgetting" that has made the various Creole dialects so fragile—in comparison to the languages composing them, especially French wherever it is in authority, as in Guadeloupe and Martinique.

69

able to the particular situation of the Plantation in the Caribbean and the Indian Ocean.

Then delusion. Unlike this oral and popular literature, though equally discontinuous, another, written and elitist literature developed. The colonists and the Planters, as well as the travelers who visited them, were possessed of a real need to justify the system. To fantasize legitimacy. And, of course, this is why, unlike what happened in the oral texts, the description of reality would turn out to be indispensable to them—and irrefutable in their terms. Reality was fantasized here as well, its image the product of a disguised apology rather than that of an austere realism. One condition of the process was that conventional landscape be pushed to extremes—the gentleness and beauty of it—particularly in the islands of the Caribbean. There is something of an involuntary Parnassus in the novels and pamphlets written by colonists of Santo Domingo and Martinique: the same propensity to blot out the shudders of life, that is, the turbulent realities of the Plantation, beneath the conventional splendor of scenery.

Another convention provided the occasion for a specific category of writing. The supposedly receptive lasciviousness of the slaves, mulatto women and men who were of mixed blood, and the animal savagery with which the Africans were credited, produced an abundant supply for the erotic literature flourishing in the islands from the seventeenth to the end of the nineteenth century. In this manner, from one blind spot to the next, a literature of illusion came into being, one moreover that, every now and then, was not lacking charm or an old-fashioned grace. Lafcadio Hearn, an international reporter and a writer as well, came from Louisiana to the Antilles at the turn of the century, sending us a much embellished report.

Memory. After the System collapsed the literatures that had asserted themselves within its space developed, for the most

70

part, from the general traits so sketchily indicated here, either consenting to them or taking an opposite course. Thus, Caribbean literatures, whether in English, Spanish, or French, tended to introduce obscurities and breaks—like so many detours—into the material they dealt with; putting into practice, like the Plantation tales, processes of intensification, breathlessness, digression, and immersion of individual psychology within the drama of a common destiny. The symbolism of situations prevailed over the refinement of realisms, by encompassing, transcending, and shedding light upon it. This, of course, is equally true of a writer of Creole such as the Haitian Franketienne as of a novelist from the United States such as Toni Morrison.

So, too, the works that appeared in these countries went against the convention of a falsely legitimizing landscape scenery and conceived of landscape as basically implicated in a story, in which it too was a vivid character.

So, finally, historical *marronage* intensified over time to exert a creative *marronage*, whose numerous forms of expression began to form the basis for a continuity. Which made it no longer possible to consider these literatures as exotic appendages of a French, Spanish, or English literary corpus; rather, they entered suddenly, with the force of a tradition that they built themselves, into the relation of cultures.

But the truth is that their concern, its driving force and hidden design, is the derangement of the memory, which determines, along with imagination, our only way to tame time.

Just how were our memory and our time buffeted by the Plantation? Within the space apart that it comprised, the always multilingual and frequently multiracial tangle created inextricable knots within the web of filiations, thereby breaking the clear, linear order to which Western thought had imparted such brilliance. So Alejo Carpentier and Faulkner are of the same mind, Edward Kamau Brathwaite and Lezama Lima go together, I recognize myself in Derek Wal-

71

cott, we take delight in the coils of time in García Márquez's century of solitude. The ruins of the Plantation have affected American cultures all around.

And, whatever the value of the explanations or the publicity Alex Haley afforded us with *Roots,* we have a strong sense that the overly certain affiliation invoked there does not really suit the vivid genius of our countries. Memory in our works is not a calendar memory; our experience of time does not keep company with the rhythms of month and year alone; it is aggravated by the void, the final sentence of the Plantation; our generations are caught up within an extended family in which our root stocks have diffused and everyone had two names, an official one and an essential one—the nickname given by his community. And when in the end it all began to shift, or rather collapse, when the unstoppable evolution had emptied the enclosure of people to reassemble them in the margins of cities, what remained, what still remains, is the dark side of this impossible memory, which has a louder voice and one that carries farther than any chronicle or census.

The disintegration of the system left its marks. Almost everywhere planter castes degenerated into fixed roles, in which memory no longer functioned except as decor—as landscape had formerly done. Occasionally, they were able to switch to commerce; otherwise, they went to pieces in melancholy. Former employees here and there formed groups of so-called poor whites, who fed the ideologies of racist terror. In the Caribbean and in Latin America the burgeoning shantytowns drew masses of the destitute and transformed the rhythm of their voices. In the islands black and Hindu farmers went to war against arbitrariness and absolute poverty. In the United States southern blacks went up North, following the "underground railroad," toward cities that were becoming violently dehumanized, where, nonetheless the Harlem writers, for example, wrote their Renaissance upon the walls of solitude. Thus, urban literature made its appearance in Bahia, New York, Jacmel, or Fort-de-France. The Plantation region, having joined with the endless terrain of haciendas or latifundio, spread thin to end up in mazes of sheet metal and concrete in which our common future takes its chances. This second Plantation matrix, after that of the slave ship, is where we must return to track our difficult and opaque sources.

3

It is not just literature. When we examine how speech functions in this Plantation realm, we observe that there are several almost codified types of expression. Direct, elementary speech, articulating the rudimentary language necessary to get work done; stifled speech, corresponding to the silence of this world in which knowing how to read and write is forbidden; deferred or disguised speech, in which men and women who are gagged keep their words close. The Creole language integrated these three modes and made them jazz.

It is understandable that in this universe every cry was an event. Night in the cabins gave birth to this other enormous silence from which music, inescapable, a murmur at first, finally burst out into this long shout—a music of reserved spirituality through which the body suddenly expresses itself. Monotonous chants, syncopated, broken by prohibitions, set free by the entire thrust of bodies, produced their language from one end of this world to the other. These musical expressions born of silence: Negro spirituals and blues, persisting in towns and growing cities; jazz, *biguines,* and calypsos, bursting into barrios and shantytowns; salsas and reggaes, assembled everything blunt and direct, painfully stifled, and patiently differed into this varied speech. This was the cry of the Plantation, transfigured into the speech of the world.

73

For three centuries of constraint had borne down so hard that, when this speech took root, it sprouted in the very midst of the field of modernity; that is, it grew for everyone. This is the only sort of universality there is: when, from a specific enclosure, the deepest voice cries out.

4

Negative explanations for what is unique to the system are clear: the decisive impact of the African population, but with the horrors of the slave trade as its beginning; the grasping opposition to change inherent in pro-slavery assumptions; the dependent relationship with the outside world that all Plantations had in common.

But one can also see how this monstrously abortive failure, composed of so many solitary instances of sterility, had a positive effect on some portion of contemporary histories. — How? is your question. How can you claim that such an anomaly could have contributed to what you call modernity? —I believe I have answered this question or at least left clues about how it may be answered.

The Plantation, like a laboratory, displays most clearly the opposed forces of the oral and the written at work—one of the most deep-rooted topics of discussion in our contemporary landscape. It is there that multilingualism, that threatened dimension of our universe, can be observed for one of the first times, organically forming and disintegrating. It is also within the Plantation that the meeting of cultures is most clearly and directly observable, though none of the inhabitants had the slightest hint that this was really about a clash of cultures. Here we are able to discover a few of the formational laws of the cultural *métissage* that concerns us all. It is essential that we investigate historicity—that conjunction of a passion for self-definition and an obsession with time that is also one of the ambitions of contemporary literatures—in the extensions of the Plantation, in the things to which it gave birth at the very instant it vanished as a functional unit. *Baroque speech, inspired by all possible speech,* was ardently created in these same extensions and loudly calls out to us from them. The Plantation is one of the bellies of the world, not the only one, one among so many others, but it has the advantage of being able to be studied with the utmost precision. Thus, the boundary, its structural weakness, becomes our advantage. And in the end its seclusion has been conquered. The place was closed, but the word derived from it remains open. This is one part, a limited part, of the lesson of the world.

# Concerning a Baroque Abroad in the World

The baroque made its appearance in the West at a moment when a particular idea of Nature—as harmonious, homogeneous, and thoroughly knowable—was in force. Rationalism refined this conception, one convenient to its own increasing ambition to master reality. At the same time, the spectacle of Nature was supposedly something one could reproduce: knowledge and imitation set themselves up as mutual guarantors.

The ideal of imitation presupposed that beneath the appearance of things, but basic to them, there lay the same "depth," some indubitable truth, led to primarily by the sciences and more closely represented in art, to the extent that these representations systematized their reproductions of reality and recognized the legitimacy of its aesthetic. Thus, the revolution in perspective in paintings from the beginnings of the Quattrocento was conceived of as moving toward this depth.

Against this tendency a baroque "rerouting" emerged and thrived. Baroque art was a reaction against the rationalist pretense of penetrating the mysteries of the known with one uniform and conclusive move. A baroque shudder, via this rerouting, set out to convey that all knowledge is to come and that this is what makes it of value. Baroque techniques, moreover, would favor "expansion" over "depth."

This historically determined rerouting generated a new heroism in the approach to knowledge, a stubborn renouncement of any ambition to summarize the world's matter in sets of imitative harmonies that would approach some essence. Baroque art mustered bypasses, proliferation, spatial redundancy, anything that flouted the alleged unicity of the thing known and the knowing of it, anything exalting quantity infinitely resumed and totality infinitely ongoing.

The "historical" baroque constituted, thus, a reaction against so-called natural order, naturally fixed as obvious fact. As conceptions of nature evolved and, at the same time, the world opened up for Western man, the baroque impulse also became generalized. The baroque, the art of expansion, expanded in concrete terms.

The first account of this was Latin American religious art, so close to Iberian or Flemish baroque but so closely intermingled with autochthonous tones boldly introduced into the baroque concert. These elements do not occur as innovations in the representation of reality but as novel bits of information concerning a nature that was definitely "new." Baroque art ceased its adversarial role; it established an innovative vision (soon a different conception) of Nature and acted in keeping with it.

This evolution reached its high point in *métissage*. Through its vertiginous styles, languages and cultures hurtled the baroque will. The generalization of *métissage* was all that the baroque needed to become naturalized. From then on what it expressed in the world was the proliferating contact of diversified natures. It grasped, or rather gave-on-and-with, this movement of the world. No longer a reaction, it was the outcome of every aesthetic, or every philosophy. Consequently, it asserted not just an art or a style but went beyond this to produce a being-in-the-world.

Contemporary conceptions of the sciences encountered and confirmed this expanding baroque. Science, of course, postulated that reality could not be defined on the basis of its appearance, that it was necessary to penetrate into its "depths," but it also agreed that knowledge of these was always deferred, that no longer were there grounds for claiming to discover the essentials all of a piece. Science entered an age of rational and basic uncertainties. That is, the conceptions of Nature expanded, became relative, which is the very basis of the baroque tendency.

Conceptions of human nature were no longer based upon a transparent model that was universally grounded or that could be universally embodied. Being-in-the-world is nothing without the quantified totality of every sort of being-in-society. Nor is it a cultural, irrefutable model. All human cultures have experienced a classicism, an age of dogmatic certitude, one that henceforth all must transcend together. And every culture, at one time or another in its development, has contrived baroque disturbances against this certainty. And each transcendence of this certainty was prophesied and simultaneously made possible by means of these disturbances. In this full-sense the "depths" illuminated by Western science, psychology, and sociology are in refutation of "depth," sensed by this same West's classicism alone. Therein lies the movement of the baroque spreading into the world.

We can sum this up: the baroque has undergone a naturalization, not just as art and style but as a way of living the unity-diversity of the world. This process of naturalization prolongs the baroque and recreates it, beyond the flamboyant realms of a unique Counter-Reformation, to extend it into the unstable mode of Relation; and, once again in this full-sense, the "historical" baroque prefigured, in an astonishingly prophetic manner, present-day upheavals of the world.

# Concerning the Poem's Information

Some critical minds, more given to talk than to analysis, proclaim or prophesy the obsolescence of poetry as no longer corresponding to the conditions of contemporary life and somehow outmoded in relation to the violence and haste abundant in modernity.[1] This traditional debate has been going on ever since reason, in the Western sense, apparently dissociated poetic creation (deemed useless in the city-state) and scientific knowledge (strictly inscribed within the drama of its own evolution). The question remains always the same, in the same context: What's the use of poetry? Modern works have already given their answer, from Rimbaud to Claudel or Aimé Césaire: Poetry is not an amusement nor a display of sentiments or beautiful things. It also imparts form to a knowledge that could never be stricken by obsolescence.

Poets today, fascinated by the adventure of computers [*l'informatique*], sense that here lies, if not the germ of a possible response to society's haranguing, at least a chance to reconnect the two orders of knowledge, the poetic and the scientific. Visible now, and approachable thanks to computers, scientific intention, putting in action the most obvious workings of social responsibility, concretely alerts and questions the poet. For what information can the poem be responsible? Can this information shoot through a computer's laser jets, something really more serious than the game of skittles that Malherbe evoked years ago?

81

The first observation, concerning the relationship between poetry and computers, revolves around an obvious difference: the binary character of the latter. Binarity is not a simple one-two rhythm, but neither is it a poetic mode, in every instance inferring something original or revealed. Accident that is not the result of chance is natural to poems, whereas it is the consummate vice (the "virus") of any self-enclosed system, such as the computer.*

The poet's truth is also the desired truth of the other, whereas, precisely, the truth of a computer system is closed back upon its own sufficient logic. Moreover, every conclusion reached by such a system has been inscribed in the original data, whereas poetics open onto unpredictable and unheard of things.

That is to say that exclusion is the rule in binary practice (either/or), whereas poetics aims for the space of difference—not exclusion but, rather, where difference is realized in going beyond.

The advent of computers has, nonetheless, thrown poetics into reverse. By making speed commonplace. Just as romantic parallels or daring surrealist images now are displayed in contemporary production of publicity "spots" and music videos, the sudden flash, the poetics of the moment, has become established and in some ways obliterated within the unimaginable instantaneousness of the computer.

As if in preparation for such a shock, three poetic works have already been composed as systems: Mallarmé's *Un coup de dés jamais n'abolira le hasard* (Dice Thrown Never Will Annul Chance), Joyce's *Finnegan's Wake,* and Ezra Pound's *Cantos.* In these works a poetics of duration, as full of revelations as the poetics of the moment, began once more to be explored. Renounced first and foremost in Mallarmé's search for the absolute, Joyce's search for totality, and

*No matter how much diversity there is in the variables created within such a system, it is always dependent on information stored in a yes/no/yes form.

82

Pound's search for multiplicity was Rimbaud's magnificent claim concerning the sudden flash of revelation.

Every computer system, through its very instantaneity, makes us familiar with unilingual revelation and renders the sudden flash ordinary—but, from the viewpoint of a multilingual scintillation, the aforementioned system is incapable of "comprehending."

Imagine a young man oblivious to anything that is not his machine; before it he is absolutely "deranged in his senses" [*déréglé des sens*], a hoodlum afar and a saint at his desk, one who has conquered the mechanics of vowels and consonants and penetrated their color: a computer scientist but also Rimbaud. The latter went after the most raging fulguration, speed's sole music, and left room for the versions of patience that Mallarmé stitched together, Joyce synthesized, and Pound derived.

These poets had a premonition: of a tremendous unknown lying ahead of us, with its demand that the totality be conveyed, that is, finally, the speech of all peoples, the ring of every language. The computer scientist will exclaim that his machine, better than any other possible, sets us to thinking of totality. But his is a totality deciphered through a game of signs, a code totality. It evades the drama of languages.

(That the necessity for using computers today brings with it writing's obituary has been sufficiently discussed. Maybe, in fact, we will soon be the threatened disciples of a catacomb religion, uniting in secret away from public prosecution and punishment, to celebrate damned masses of writing, to communicate by sharing texts otherwise impossible to find or objectionable. Are computers the harbingers of such perdition?)

But the drama does not simply boil down to a possible deathblow for writing. Now the crisis of writing as a form of expression meets the sudden burgeoning of oral languages. Are we perhaps witnessing a transitional passage here? Yesterday we distinguished between the oral and the written, with the latter being transcendent. Maybe tomorrow we shall be living through a synthesis that could be summed up as the written resolution, or transcription onto the page (which is our screen), of an economy of orality. This is the passage opening onto the archipelago of languages.

Oral forms of poetry are multiplying, giving rise to ceremonies, performances, and shows. All around the world—in the Antilles, in the Americas, in Africa and Asia—poets of the spoken word savor this turnaround, which mixes the jangling brilliance of oral rhetoric into the alchemy of written words. Poetic knowledge is no longer inseparable from writing; momentary flashes verge on rhythmic amassings and the monotonies of duration. The sparkle of many languages utterly fulfills its function in such an encounter, in which the lightning of poetry is recreated in time's gasp.

Triggered by a premonition of this encounter between the oral and the written, many people have either a fascination with computers or merely a curiosity to see them cough up poetry. An introduction and invitation to binary speed for the operator's lasting benefit. A roll of the dice endlessly resumed. Systematics simultaneously stitched together, synthesized, and derived. But missing throughout will be the vivid contrast among the languages of the world. Which constitutes the desiring flesh of a poem.

The computer, on the other hand, seems to be the privileged instrument of someone wanting to "follow" any Whole whose variants multiply vertiginously. It is useful for suggesting what is stable within the unstable. Therefore, though it does not create poetry, it can "show the way" to a poetics.

Even so, despite its high visibility, this machine is not the place in which science and poetry might connect. This place precedes any technique of application; it generates its space within the indeterminacy of axioms.

Poetic thought, before or after the accident of the poem, or through it, attempts to set itself up in an axiomatic system: to knit something up whose stitches won't run. That creates the opportunity for an infinite sort of conjunction, in which science and poetry are equivalent. Here the axiom is a grounding fantasy, even if it is then perpetuated through conquests of ideas. This fantasy is privileged in not having to be either elucidated or resorbed; the psychoanalysis of knowledge is fixed on something else entirely. The poetic axiom, like the mathematical axiom, is illuminating because it is fragile and inescapable, obscure and revealing. In both instances the prospective system accepts the accident and grasps that in the future it will be transcended. Science transforms its languages; poetry invents its tongues. For neither is it a question of exploring, but one, rather, of going toward a totality that is unrealizable, without being required to say where they will come together—nor even that they have any need to do so.

III

# PATHS

*Out loud, to mark the split*

# CREOLIZATIONS

*Creolization, one of the ways of forming a complex mix—and not merely a linguistic result—is only exemplified by its processes and certainly not by the "contents" on which these operate. This is where we depart from the concept of creoleness. Though this notion covers (no more and no less) that which accounts for creolizations, it goes on to propose two further extensions. The first opens onto a broader ethnocultural realm, from the Antilles to the Indian Ocean. But variations of this sort do not seem to be determining factors, because the speed with which they change in Relation is so great. The second is an attempt to get at Being. But that would constitute a step backward in comparison with how creolizations can function. We propose neither humanity's Being nor its models. We are not prompted solely by the defining of our identities but by their relation to everything possible as well— the mutual mutations generated by this interplay of relations. Creolizations bring into Relation but not to universalize; the principles of creoleness regress toward negritudes, ideas of Frenchness, of Latinness, all generalizing concepts—more or less innocently.*

# Dictate, Decree

Baroque derangement and the guarantee provided by scientific rigor: just yesterday these were the counterpoises of our movement (our *balan,* our surge, our momentum) toward *totalité-monde.*[1]

But the baroque no longer constitutes a derangement, since it has turned into a "natural" expression of whatever scatters and comes together. The age of classicisms (of deepening an internal unity, raised to the dimensions of a universal itself postulated) is past, no doubt, for all cultures. It remains to make the network of their convergences work, or to untangle it. It remains to study those cultures that have not had time, before coming into planetary contact (or conflict), to realize "their own" classicism. Are their powers not impeded as they come to the meeting? Then again, what shall we say about composite cultures, whose composition did not result from a union of "norms" but, rather, was built in the margins with all kinds of materials that by their very nature were exceptions to the patience of the rule, to be thrust headlong into the world by necessity, oppression, anguish, greed, or an appetite for adventure?

The baroque is the favored speech of these cultures, even if henceforth it belongs to all. We call it baroque, because we know that confluences always partake of marginality, that classicisms partake of intolerance, and that, for us, the substitute for the hidden violence of these intolerant exclusions is the manifest and integrating violence of contaminations.

Note that *métissage* exists in places where categories making their essences distinct were formerly in opposition. The more *métissage* became realized, the more the idea of it faded. As the baroque became naturalized in the world, it tended to become a commonplace, a generality (which is not the same as a generalization), of a new regime. Because it proliferated rather than deepened a norm, it is unable to consent to "classicisms." There is no culture rightfully impeded in the baroque; none imposes its tradition, even if there are some that export their generalizing products everywhere.

How can continuity (which is "desirable") be practiced in this incessant turnover? How can the stabilizing action of former classicisms be replaced? And with what?

At first our only recourse in the matter seemed to be the positivity of scientific method. This, for example, was the method adopted for the defense and promotion of languages, corresponding to the ambition of linguistics to set itself up as a science. A profitable pretense: despite its failure to be confirmed, it provided the basis for a system and gathered together its scattered materials. But science had ceased having any desire to obtain this sort of guarantee, having, meanwhile, ventured not outside the positive but beyond positivism. It had come face to face with the baroque and understood that the work of the latter deserved cognizance.

The most recent developments of science invite us, therefore, to venture in our quest beyond the laws laid down by its philosophies. For a long time we have divined both order and disorder in the world and projected these as measure and excess. But every poetics led us to believe something that, of course, is not wrong: that excessiveness of order and a measured disorder exist as well. The only discernible stabilities in Relation have to do with the interdependence of the cycles operative there, how their corresponding patterns of movement are in tune. In Relation analytic thought is led to construct unities whose interdependent variances jointly piece together the interactive totality. These unities are not models but revealing *echos-monde*. Thought makes music.

William Faulkner's work, Bob Marley's song, the theories of Benoit Mandelbrot, are all *échos-monde*. Wilfredo Lam's painting (flowing together) or that of Roberto Matta (tearing apart); the architecture of Chicago and just as easily the shantytowns of Rio or Caracas; Ezra Pound's *Cantos* but also the marching of schoolchildren in Soweto are *échos-monde*.

*Finnegan's Wake* was an *écho-monde* that was prophetic and consequently absolute (without admission into the real).

Antonin Artaud's words constitute an *écho-monde* outside of the world.

Whatever, coming from a tradition, enters into Relation; whatever, defending a tradition, justifies Relation; whatever, having left behind or refuted every tradition, provides the basis for another full-sense to Relation; whatever, born of Relation, contradicts and embodies it. Anglo-American pidgin (something, therefore, spoken neither by the English nor by the Americans) is a negative *écho-monde*, whose concrete force weaves the folds of Relation and neutralizes its subsistence.

The Creole language is a fragile and revealing *écho-monde*, born of a reality of relation and limited within this reality by its dependence.

Spoken languages, without exception, have become *échos-monde*, whose lack we are only just beginning to feel each time one is wiped out by this circularity in evolution.

*Echos-monde* are not exacerbations that result directly from the convulsive conditions of Relation. They are at work in the matter of the world; they prophesy or illuminate it, divert it or conversely gain strength within it.

In order to cope with or express confluences, every individual, every community, forms its own *échos-monde*, imagined from power or vainglory, from suffering or impatience. Each individual makes this sort of music and each community as well. As does the totality composed of individuals and communities.

*Echos-monde* thus allow us to sense and cite the cultures of peoples in the turbulent confluence whose globality organizes our *chaos-monde*. They pattern its constituent (not conclusive) elements and its expressions.

What we earlier remarked in Saint-John Perse as an aesthetics of the universe ("narration of the universe"), we now describe in a different manner. It is an aesthetics of the *chaos-monde*.

The *chaos-monde* is only disorder if one assumes there to be an order whose full force poetics is not prepared to reveal (poetics is not a science). The ambition of poetics, rather, is to safeguard the energy of this order. The aesthetics of the universe assumed preestablished norms; the aesthetics of *chaos-monde* is the impassioned illustration and refutation of these. Chaos is not devoid of norms, but these neither constitute a goal nor govern a method there.

*Chaos-monde* is neither fusion nor confusion: it acknowledges neither the uniform blend—a ravenous integration—nor muddled nothingness. Chaos is not "chaotic."

But its hidden order does not presuppose hierarchies or pre-cellencies—neither of chosen languages nor of princenations. The *chaos-monde* is not a mechanism; it has no keys.

The aesthetics of the *chaos-monde* (what we were thus calling the aesthetics of the universe but cleared of a priori values) embraces all the elements and forms of expression of this totality within us; it is totality's act and its fluidity, totality's reflection and agent in motion.

The baroque is the not-established outcome of this motion.

Relation is that which simultaneously realizes and expresses this motion. It is the *chaos-monde* relating (to itself).

The poetics of Relation (which is, therefore, part of the aesthetics of the *chaos-monde*) senses, assumes, opens, gathers,

94

scatters, continues, and transforms the thought of these elements, these forms, and this motion.

Destructure these facts, declare them void, replace them, reinvent their music: totality's imagination is inexhaustible and always, in every form, wholly legitimate—that is, free of all legitimacy.

An equilibrium and ability to endure are revived through *échos-monde*. Individuals and communities go beyond vainglory or suffering, power or impatience, together—however imperceptibly. The important thing is that such a process represents an optimum. Its results are unpredictable, but the beginnings of the capacity to endure are detectible, coming where formerly there were classicisms. It is no longer through deepening a tradition but through the tendency of all traditions to enter into relation that this is achieved. Baroques serve to relay classicisms. Techniques of relation are gradually substituted for techniques of the absolute, which frequently were techniques of self-absolution. The arts of expanse relate (dilate) the arts of depth.

These are the forms we must use to contemplate the evolution of the Creole language: viewing it as a propagation of the dialects that compose it, each extending toward the other; but being aware also that this language can disappear, or un-appear if you will, in one place or another.

We agree that the extinction of any language at all impoverishes everyone. And even more so, if that is possible, when a composite language like Creole is in question, for this would be an instant setback for the processes of bringing-into-relation. But how many languages, dialects, or idioms will have vanished, eroded by the implacable consensus among powers between profits and controls, before human communities learn to preserve together their diversities. The threat of this disappearance is one of the facts to be incorporated, as we earlier remarked, into the field of descriptive linguistics.

95

Not every disappearance, however, is equivalent. The fact that French-Ontarians are gradually ceasing to speak French will not cause the latter to vanish from the world panorama. Creole is not in the same situation because its elision in one single region would make the areas of its survival even more scarce. But establishing that these differences exist in no way attenuates both the human drama unleashed each time it happens and the extent of impoverishment then inflicted upon the *chaos-monde.*

We are not going to save one language or another here or there, while letting others perish. The floodtide of extinction, unstoppable in its power of contagion, will win out. It will leave a residue that is not one victorious language, or several, but one or more desolate codes that will take a long time to reconstitute the organic and unpredictable liveliness of a language. Linguistic multiplicity protects ways of speaking, from the most extensive to the most fragile. It is in the name of this total multiplicity and in function of it, rather than of any selective pseudo-solidarities, that each language must be defended.

An idiom like Creole, one so rapidly constituted in so fluid a field of relations, cannot be analyzed the way, for example, it was done for Indo-European languages that aggregated slowly around their roots. We need to know why this Creole language was the only one to appear, why it took the same forms in both the Caribbean basin and the Indian Ocean, and why solely in countries colonized by the French; whereas the other languages of this colonization process, English and Spanish, remained inflexible as far as the colonized populations were concerned, their only concessions being pidgins or other dialects that were derived.*

*Another language of the region that would be an exception to this statistical rule is Papiamento, which has a Spanish lexical basis in countries (Curaçao) that are no longer Spanish. It seems that, in this same region of the Americas, more and more linguistic microzones are being discovered in which Creoles, pidgins, and patois become undifferentiated.

One possible response—in any case, the one I venture—is that the French language, which we think of as so intent on universality, was, of course, not like this at the time of the conquest of the Americas, having perhaps not yet achieved its normative unity. Breton and Norman dialects, the ones used in Santo Domingo and the other islands, were less coercively centripetal and thus able to enter into the composition of a new language. English and Spanish were already perhaps more "classic," and lent themselves less to this first amalgam from which a language could have sprung. Of course, the "unified" French language also spread throughout these territories with no language. The Creole compromise (metaphorical and synthesizing), favored by Plantation structure, was the result of both the uprooting of African languages and the deviance of French provincial idioms. The origins of this compromise are already a marginality. It did, indeed, name another reality, another mentality; but its actual poetics—or construction—was what was deviant in relation to any supposed classicism.

Traditional linguistics, when applied to such a case, seeks first and foremost (and counter to what the history of the language would indicate) to "classify" this language. That is—and it is perfectly understandable—it attempts to endow it with a body of rules and specifically stated standards ensuring its ability to endure. But, though fixing usage and transcription are both indispensable, there still remains a need to devise (given marginality as a component of the language) systems of variables, such as I earlier discussed, that would be distinguished from a mere allocation of variants among the dialects—of Haiti, Guadeloupe, or Guiana, etc.—of this Creole language. We would have a whole range of choices within each dialect. Wherever etymology or phonetics faltered (and, doubtless, etymology would be of less use in the matter) one should let poetics take its course, that is, follow intuition about both the history of the language and its development in the margins. In other words, the alleged scientific character can lapse into scholarly illusion, can conceal its stratagem

97

for "staying put." The standard of such a language formation would be fluent. One could never legitimately have decreed it.

The decisive element, as far as fixing language is concerned, is the rule of usage; those who forge words frequently come up against it. And, in turn, this rule depends to a large extent on the practical functioning of the language. But, in the environment we have outlined (combining *échos-monde* and prevalent baroque), one could assume that the true basis for an ability to endure is that the rule of usage have both momentum and diffraction.

One can imagine language diasporas that would change so rapidly within themselves and with such feedback, so many turnarounds of norms (deviations and back and forth) that their fixity would lie in that change. Their ability to endure would not be accessible through deepening but through the shimmer of variety. It would be a fluid equilibrium. This linguistic sparkle, so far removed from the mechanics of sabirs and codes, is still inconceivable for us, but only because we are paralyzed to this day by monolingual prejudice ("my language is my root").

The normative decree, edict and instrument of this prejudice, prides itself, then, on the outmoded "guarantees" of scientific positivism and tries to administer the evolution of threatened languages, such as Creole, by attempting to "furnish" such a guarantee to the principle of identity (of permanence) that language implies. But it is not simply because the Creole language is a component of my identity that I am worried about its possible disappearance; it is because the language would also be missing from the radiant sparkle, the fluid equilibrium, and the ability to endure in disorder of the *chaos-monde*. The way that I defend it must take this into account.

Normative decrees have ceased to be the authoritative rule as far as vehicular languages are concerned. English and Spanish, the most massive of these, and seemingly the best entrenched in a sort of continental nature, met on the territory of the United States (Puerto Ricans, Chicanos, the immigrants in Florida). It may well be that their massiveness has become fissured, that alongside the variances proliferating Anglo-American, lucky contaminations from the Spanish will occur, and vice versa. This process will no doubt move more quickly than any analysis one will be able to make of it.

Contemporary arguments over whether or not to simplify the spelling of the French language demonstrate how many contaminations have occurred there. These proposals are a counter-decree, as futile as the purism they oppose is inoperative. Though the language must change in the world, and its plurality must be confirmed, only dictions will bring this about—not some authoritative edict.

We can only follow from afar the experimentation feeling its way along in all the elsewheres that we dream of.* Is the Chinese language absorbing the Latin alphabet? How is the actual status of languages changing in the Soviet Union? Is Quechuan beginning to make its escape from silence? And in Europe are the Scandinavian languages starting to open up to the world? Are forms of creolization silently at work, and where? Will Swahili and Fulani share the written domain with other languages in Africa? Are regional dialects in France fading away? How quickly? Will ideograms, pictograms, and other forms of writing show up in this panorama? Do translations already allow perceptible correspondences between

*It is not essential to note that archipelagic agglomerations of language have formed everywhere. Either according to "roots" or families: Indo-European languages, Latin languages, etc. Or according to their characteristic techniques of relation: composite languages, Creole languages, etc. Or according to both dimensions at once: vehicular languages and their pidgins, all languages and their dialects, etc. It is dangerous for the world's poetic diversity merely to link each of these agglomerations to some politically self-interested project. What is important is to track down the constants both within the agglomerations and within the majority of their confluences: Is there a hidden order to contacts among languages?

language systems? And how many minorities are there struggling within diglossia, like the numerous French-speaking Creole blacks in southwestern Louisiana? Or the thirty thousand Inuits on Baffin Island? Lists of this sort are not innocent; they accustom the mind to apprehending problems in a circular manner and to hatching solutions interdependently. Relating realms of knowledge (questions and solutions) with one another cannot be categorized as either a discipline or a science but, rather, as an imaginary construct of reality that permits us to escape the pointillistic probability approach without lapsing into abusive generalization.

The pronouncement of decrees in any case (issuing edicts that constrict the future of the language) does not set you free from collective anxieties. Game shows on television, organized in every country equipped to do so, spotlight the destabilization of languages in a spectacular manner. These games are the same everywhere. One must reconstitute words whose letters are either hidden or given in no order. Meaning has little importance, and there have been cases in which contestants have appeared on the shows after having learned whole sections of dictionary. So one disjoints a language, taking into account, in short, only its skeleton (if one can speak of the lexicon as a mere skeleton) to which one clings.

The amusing character of these exercises, which fall within the province of true performance, links them with another sort of contest that is organized in France on a very large scale and whose purpose is a much more elitist practice: dictation. The dictation is diction doing its best. In it, of course, it is a matter of conquering the difficulties of French syntax and grammar, which, as everyone knows, are not simple.

Thus, a learning exercise, whose success depended on its repetition day after day (we all remember the fateful dictation period in primary school), has turned into a show. Where we had to learn, now we have to win. To prove there are people, beginning with the winners of these sparring matches, who still are interested in the subtleties—even the most specious—of the language and who more often than not master these.

These games seem to me a nostalgic exercise not devoid of a strong tinge of collective anxiety.

Dictating, decreeing: both activities (in their secret complicity: a decree affixes laws to us, a dictation is from an edict now essential) attempt to form a dam against what makes languages fragile—contaminations, slovenliness, barbarism.

But what you would call barbarism is the inexhaustible motion of the scintillations of languages, heaving dross and inventions, dominations and accords, deathly silences and irrepressible explosions, along with them. These languages combine, vary, clash, so rapidly that the lengthy training of earlier times is no longer worth much. Decreeing will have to use dialects, devise systems of variables. Dictation, if it exists, will have to transform itself into an exercise in creation, with no obligation or penalty. Faults of syntax are, for the moment, less decisive than faults of relation (though they may be symptoms among others of the latter) and will take less time to correct. On the other hand, let's admit to taking a very personal pleasure in these rules when they improve the quality of our expression. The only merit to correctness of language lies in what this language says in the world: even correctness is variable.

Baroque naturalities and the forms of *chaos-monde* have a (desirable) ability to endure that a priori reasoning will not unearth. It will not precede their work, the movement of engagement (ascendency and surprise) from which, simultaneously, their matter and their full-sense arise. No topology results from the *échos-monde*. But, on the other hand, the baroque is not just passion and mystery, nor does the guarantee of scientific rigor lapse in every instance into a dogma secure in the positive. Baroque naturality, if it exists, has a structure or at least an order, and we have to invent a knowledge that would not serve to guarantee its norm in advance but would follow excessively along to keep up with the measurable quantity of its vertiginous variances.

## To Build the Tower

"Live in seclusion or open up to the other": this was supposedly the only alternative for any population demanding the right to speak its own language. It is how inherited premises of centuries-old domination were given legitimacy. Either you speak a language that is "universal," or on its way to being so, and participate in the life of the world; or else you retreat into your particular idiom—quite unfit for sharing—in which case you cut yourself off from the world to wallow alone and sterile in your so-called identity.

However, as populations became liberated from legal (if not actual) dependencies, the view emerged that it is the language of a community that controls the main vector of its cultural identity, which in turn determines the conditions of the community's development. This viewpoint has been considered suspect and, more often than not, pernicious. During this same period all developmental processes became reduced to one exclusive type of perfection, that is, technological. Hence the puzzle: What is it that you are demanding when a language, one single language, would provide you with the key to progress?

Nations could have only one linguistic or cultural future—either this seclusion within a restrictive particularity or, conversely, dilution within a generalizing universal. This is a formidable construction, and the "oral genius" of peoples of the world urges us to burst our way out of it. The words of griots and storytellers washed up on the edges of large cities, and eroded by second-rate forms of progress, still endure. Gradually, the governments of poor countries are coming to understand that there is no single, transcendent, and enforceable model for development.

In this explosion of incredible diversity, linguistic relations have become marked by creations springing from the friction between languages, by the give-and-take of sudden innovation (for example, initiatory street languages in southern countries), and by masses of generally accepted notions as well as passive prejudices.

The assumption that was, perhaps, most crucial concerned the hierarchical division into written and oral languages. The latter were crude, unsuited to conceptualization and the acquisition of learning, incapable of guaranteeing the transmission of knowledge. The former were civilizing and allowed man to transcend his natural state, inscribing him both in permanence and in evolution.

It is true that literacy is a matter of utmost urgency in the world and that, lacking other appropriate materials, this is usually accomplished in what are called communication, or vehicular, languages. But we have come to realize that all literal literacy needs to be buttressed by a cultural literacy that opens up possibilities and allows the revival of autonomous creative forces from within, and hence "inside," the language under consideration. Development thus has linguistic stakes, with consequences that can be neither codified nor predicted.

Relationships between languages that were supposedly transcendent because written and others long kept at a level referred to, with a hint of condescension, as "oral"—these relationships I described of suddenness, unplanned adaptation, or systematic apprenticeship—have been made even more complex by both political and economic oppression.

*The relationship of domination,* consequently, is the most blatant, gaining strength in technological expansion and generalizing a neutral uniformity. Dominated languages are thus pigeonholed as folklore or technical irresponsibility. At this point a universal language, such as Esperanto, no matter how well thought out, is not the remedy. For any language that does not create, that does not hoe its own tuff, subtracts accordingly from the nongeneralizing universal.

*The relationship of fascination* has become, of course, less and less virulent, but it drove intellectual elites of "developing countries" to the reverent usage of a language of prestige that has only served them as self-impoverishment.

*Relationships of multiplicity or contagion* exist wherever mixtures explode into momentary flashes of creation, especially in the languages of young people. Purists grow indignant, and poets of Relation marvel at them. Linguistic borrowings are only injurious when they turn passive because they sanction some domination.

*Relationships of polite subservience or mockery* come about when frequent contact with tourist enclaves plays a substantial role, along with daily practices of subordination or domestic service. This tendency to promote the appearance of pidgins is swept aside by the politics of national education, when these are well conceived and carried to completion.

*Relationships of tangency* are by far the most insidious, appearing whenever there are composite languages, languages of compromise between two or more idioms—for example, the Creoles of francophone regions in the Americas or the Indian Ocean. Then the erosion of the new language must be forestalled, as it is eaten away from within through the mere weight of one of its components, which, meanwhile, becomes reinforced as an agent of domination.

*Relationships of subversion* exist when an entire community encourages some new and frequently antiestablishment usage of a language. English-speaking Caribbeans and blacks in the United States are two convincing examples in their use of the English language, as are the Quebecois in their appropriation of French.

*Relationships of intolerance* are seen, for example, in the teaching of a communication language. The language is established once and for all in its (original) history and regarded as uncompromising toward those formidable contagions to which speakers or creators from elsewhere are likely to subject it. An "atavistic fluidity" in exercising a language is deemed indispensible to its perfection, resulting in the opinion that theories concerning its learning and teaching can only be developed in the "country of origin."

Oppositions between the written and the oral do not date from the recent past alone; they have long exercised their divisions within a given language voice [*langue*], Arabic for example, in which two separate orders of language use [*langage*][1] for the community are designated: one learned and the other popular.

This is the case for monolingual countries with "internal" problems, in which these two usages—oral and written—introduce ruptures (through social discrimination, which deploys the rules of language usage). Other internal problems are linked, sometimes to the erosion of regional dialects inscribed within the language, sometimes to the difficulty of transcribing this language. This example provides a glimpse of the inexhaustible variety of linguistic situations—something far more unsettling than the number of spoken languages in the world.

Monolingual countries with "external" problems would be those in which a national language, the main form of communication, is threatened on an economic and cultural level by a foreign language.

In bilingual countries with internal problems there are two languages of wide communication that confront each other; each one is assumed by one portion of the community, which is destabilized in consequence.

In diglot countries one communication language tends to dominate or restrict one or several "mother tongues," vernaculars or composite languages whose tradition is oral—sometimes to the point of extinction. The tasks of fixing and transposing these languages then becomes critical. As scholars take responsibility for them and everyone uses them, these languages will doubtless reinforce compromise solutions that will spread gradually according to systems of variables. One can expect the same urgent situation to apply to languages whose writing is not phonetic, even when vigorously backed by national unanimity.

In multilingual countries with no apparent problems there is a federative principle that tempers the relations among the languages in usage, which are usually vehicular.

There are some multilingual countries, on the other hand, in which the great number of mother tongues makes choice difficult, when it comes to deciding which is the official or national language.

All these situations intersect; they add up and thwart one another and go far beyond any conflict solely between the oral and the written. They are astounding indicators of the relations among peoples and cultures. Their complexity prohibits any summary or reductive evaluation concerning the strategies to be implemented. In global relations languages work, of course, in obedience to laws of economic and political domination but elude, nonetheless, any harsh and rigid long-term forecast.

This same complexity is what allows us to come out of seclusion. We stop believing that we are alone in the sufferings of our expression. We discover that it is the same for any number of other communities.* From that point on the idea grows that speaking one's language and opening up to the language of the other no longer form the basis for an alternative. "I speak to you in your language voice, and it is in my language use that I understand you." Creating in any given language thus assumes that one be inhabited by the impossi-

---

*To our astonishment we also discover people comfortably established within the placid body of their language, who cannot even comprehend that somewhere someone might experience an agony of language and who will tell you flat out, as they have in the United States, "That is not a problem."

ble desire for all the languages in the world. Totality calls out to us. Every work of literature today is inspired by it.[2]

The fact remains, nonetheless, that, when a people speaks its language or languages, it is above all free to produce through them at every level—free, that is, to make its relationship to the world concrete and visible for itself and for others.

The defense of languages assuring Diversity is thus inseparable from restabilizing relations among communities. How is it possible to come out of seclusion if only two or three languages continue to monopolize the irrefutable powers of technology and their manipulation, which are imposed as the sole path to salvation and energized by their actual effects? This dominant behavior blocks the flowering of imaginations, forbids one to be inspired by them, and confines the general mentality within the limits of a bias for technology as the only effective approach. The long-term remedy for such losses is to spell out over and over again the notion of an ethnotechnique, by means of which choices of development would be adapted to the real needs of a community and to the protected landscape of its surroundings. Nor is it certain that this will succeed, its prospects being very chancy; but it is urgent that we take this route. The promotion of languages is the first axiom of this ethnotechnique. And we know that, in the area of understanding, poetry—watch out for it!—has always been the consummate ethnotechnique. The defense of languages can come through poetry (also).

Moreover, the tendency of all cultures to meet in a single, identical perspective laid out by radio and television unleashes yet unimagined possibilities for sharing and equality. It is not a sure thing that languages with an oral tradition would start with a disadvantage in this encounter. Perhaps more supple and adaptable, they would lend themselves to change, all the more if the only other languages are those with a written tradition, which have become stiffened and

108

fixed over the centuries. Not long ago I learned of a project in which a Japanese computer company was investing considerable sums of money on a theoretical study of several African oral languages. Its intention was to explore the capacity of these languages to generate a new computer language and to provide broad-based support for new systems. The primary goal of this research was, of course, to capture a potential market in the twenty-first century, and it was motivated by competition from Anglo-American companies. Still, it should be noted how the most self-interested technology was thereby sanctioning not the (actual) liberation of the languages of orality, of course, but already their right to be recognized.

On the other side of the bitter struggles against domination and for the liberation of the imagination, there opens up a multiply dispersed zone in which we are gripped by vertigo. But this is not the vertigo preceding apocalypse and Babel's fall. It is the shiver of a beginning, confronted with extreme possibility. It is possible to build the Tower—*in every language.*

# Transparency and Opacity

There still exist centers of domination, but it is generally acknowledged that there are no exclusive, lofty realms of learning or metropolises of knowledge left standing. Henceforward, this knowledge, composed of abstract generality and linked to the spirit of conquest and discovery, has the presence of human cultures in their solid materiality superimposed upon it. And knowledge, or at least the epistemology we produce for ourselves from it, has been changed by this. Its transparency, in fact, its legitimacy is no longer based on a Right.

Transparency no longer seems like the bottom of the mirror in which Western humanity reflected the world in its own image. There is opacity now at the bottom of the mirror, a whole alluvium deposited by populations, silt that is fertile but, in actual fact, indistinct and unexplored even today, denied or insulted more often than not, and with an insistent presence that we are incapable of not experiencing.

The recent history of the French language corresponds (and responds) to this trend. Because it lacks an anchor in areas of concrete and undisguised domination—the Anglo-American model—for some time now certain people have apparently pledged the French language to establishing a sort of semiconceptual dominance. It would thus maintain its transparency and contain the increasing opacity of the world within the limits of a well-phrased classicism, thereby perpetuating a lukewarm humanism, both colorless and reassuring.

All languages have to be defended, and therefore French (the language in which I create and, consequently, would not like to see stereotyped) must also be defended—against this sort of maladroit rearguard mission. Whether it is vehicular or not, a language that does not risk the disturbances arising from contact among cultures, and not ardently involved in the reflections generated by an equal relation with other languages, seems to me doomed to real impoverishment. It is true that the leveling effect of Anglo-American is a persistent threat for everyone and that this language, in turn, risks being transformed into a technical salesman's Esperanto, a perfunctory containerization of expression (neither Faulkner's nor Hopkins's language but not the language of London pubs or Bronx warehouses either). It is also true that the actual situation is that languages lacking the support of economic power and the competitive politics that convey this are slowly disappearing. The result is that the languages of the world, from the most prestigious to the humblest, have ended up backing the same demand, though general opinion has not yet caught up. They demand a change in ways of thinking, a break with the fatal trend to annihilate idioms, and they would grant to every language, whether powerful or not, vehicular or not, the space and means to hold its own within the total accord. It would be more beautiful to live in a symphony of languages than in some reduced universal monolingualism—neutral and standardized. There is one thing we can be sure of: a lingua franca (humanistic French, Anglo-American sabir, or Esperanto code) is always apoetical.

In the indeterminate context of the French-speaking communities we lump together as *la francophonie*, it was, therefore, an apparently simple notion to regard the French language as the a priori bearer of values that could help remedy the anarchistic tendencies of the various cultures that are, completely or partially, a product of its expression. *La francophonie* would be less what it claimed to be, an interdependent gathering of cultural convergences, than a sort of preventive medicine against cultural disintegrations and diffusions that were considered unfortunate. This is one way, at least, to analyze the discourse of a number of its early proponents.

According to this way of thinking, for example, the French language has always been inseparable from a pursuit of the dignity of mankind, insofar as man is conceived of as an irreducible entity. From this one could infer that French would thus make possible the lessening of certain angry resentments that are limiting and that have allegedly been observed in quests for identity currently taking place in the world. In a collective quest for identity—somehow now labeled the quest for ethnicity—sterile extremes would exist in which man, as an individual, would risk disappearing. Because the French language vouches for the dignity of the individual, the use of it would limit any such excesses on the part of the collectivity. In other words, this language would have a humanizing function supposedly inseparable from its very nature, which would serve as protection against the rash actions of an excessive collectivization of identity. In the present conceptual debate the French language, the language of the Rights of Man, would provide useful protection against excesses set in motion by the presuppositions of any proclamation of the Rights of Peoples. *La francophonie* would provide that transcendency by giving the correct version of humanism.

Another characteristic of the language would lie in its literary dedication to clarity, a mission that has led to its reputation for a pleasing rationality, which is, in fact, the guarantee of a legitimate pleasure to be had in the manipulation of a unity composed of consecutive, noncontradictory, concise statements.

The "essential" nature of literary language would preexist any of the felicitous or infelicitous accidents of its real, diversified cultural usages. (This literary mission repeats certain tactical approaches: the defense of languages is said to be inscribed in the nature of the French language as defined here; it is a plural *francophonie,* or, as regards the Antilles and Indian Ocean, the speaking of Creole within a French-speaking population.) Looked at this way, French would represent not just what is common in various ways to the linguistic practice of the populations constituting francophone culture, it would also, in literature, or perhaps even in absolute terms, be what is given in advance. From this it takes no time to reach the conclusion that there is a "right" way to use the language. And the natural result will be scales of value to appraise usage in the French-speaking realm.* Language would reveal the differing degrees in this hierarchical organization.**

Neither its humanizing function, however (the famous universality of French as the bearer of humanism), nor its concordant predestination to be clear (its pleasurable rationality) stand up to examination. Languages have no mission. This is, however, the sort of learnedly dealt nonsense we have to struggle eternally against in a discourse depriving populations of cultural identity. An attentive observer will notice that such windbags are anxiously intent on confining themselves to the false transparency of a world they used to run; they do not want to enter into the penetrable opacity of a world in which one exists, or agrees to exist, with and among others. In the history of the language the claim that the conciseness of French is consecutive and noncontradictory is the veil obscuring and justifying this refusal. This is, in fact, a rearguard mission.

---

*Already a distinction is made between *la francophonie* of the north, the French spoken in France, Switzerland, Belgium, or Quebec; and *la francophonie* of the south, everything else.
**Specialists in francophone literatures do not always resist "comparing" the writers from these countries. This objectifying practice negates with one stroke the organic unity of our literatures for the benefit of the appreciation of the critic, who would never dare apply such methods to the French literary corpus.

Just as there is a right way to use the language, there would be a "correct" way to teach it. This notion has repercussions not just on the idea one has of the language but on the idea one forms of its relationship with other languages. Consequently, there are also repercussions on the theoretical apparatus set in place by disciplines pertaining to language usage, whether these are used to analyze languages or to translate from one to the other or to make learning a language possible.

If, however, we look at literary texts, which after all best delineate the image of a language, if not its function, and if we analyze how such texts are affected by language learning or translation (these being the two fundamental mechanisms of relational practice), ideas of transparency and opacity quite naturally present themselves as the critical approach.

The literary text plays the contradictory role of a producer of opacity.

Because the writer, entering the dense mass of his writings, renounces an absolute, his poetic intention, full of self-evidence and sublimity. Writing's relation to that absolute is relative; that is, it actually renders it opaque by realizing it in language. The text passes from a dreamed-of transparency to the opacity produced in words.

Because the written text opposes anything that might lead a reader to formulate the author's intention differently. At the same time he can only guess at the shape of this intention. The reader goes, or rather tries to go back, from the produced opacity to the transparency that he read into it.

Literary textual practice thus represents an opposition between two opacities: the irreducible opacity of the text, even when it is a matter of the most harmless sonnet, and the always evolving opacity of the author or a reader. Sometimes the latter becomes literally conscious of this opposition, in which case he describes the text as "difficult."

Both learning a language and translation have in common

the attempt to give "some transparency" back to a text. That is, they strive to bridge two series of opacities: in the case of language learning these would be the text and the novice reader confronting it, for whom any text is supposedly difficult. In the case of translation the transparency must provide a passage from a risky text to what is possible for another text.

Preferably, the literary works one chooses for learning a language are those best corresponding to what is assumed to be the pattern of the language, not the "easiest" works but ones supposedly having the least threatening opacity. This was true of texts by Albert Camus given to foreign students in France during the 1960s—a revealing instance of fundamental misinterpretation, since Camus's work only gave the appearance of being clear and straightforward. Language learning, whose main axiom was clarity, skipped right over the situational crisis that events in Algeria had formed in Camus and the echoes of this in the tight, feverish, and restrained structure of the style he had adopted to both confide and withdraw at the same time.

When it is a question of using a language, therefore, we must analyze the "situational competence" (to use an expression of Patrick Charaudeau's) of this language. Charaudeau showed how the preliminary stages of language learning consist of bringing the student to a state of "situational competence" in relation to the subject of the text he is tackling. Extending this notion from language learning to usage, I think that there is a global situational competence that the learner as well as the speaker or author needs to be aware of and that it concerns not a given text but the language itself: its situation within Relation, its precursors and its conceivable future.[1]

So we must reevaluate vehicular languages, that is, the Western languages, which have spread practically everywhere in the world. Communities that are too "dense" to be considered as the linguistic margins of their languages' countries of origin have adopted them in their diffusion. The United States is not considered peripheral to Great Britain (and neither is Australia or Canada); nor is Brazil peripheral in relation to Portugal nor Argentina nor Mexico in relation to Spain. Among these vehicular languages only French seems to have spread everywhere without really concentrating anywhere. French-speaking Belgium and Quebec are threatened, the Maghreb becomes more and more Arabic, the African states and francophone countries in the Caribbean do not carry sufficient weight, at least in political and economic terms. Moreover, as French spread, it simultaneously strengthened the illusion that its place of origin remained (even today) the privileged womb and promoted the belief that this language had some kind of universal value that had nothing whatsoever to do with the areas into which it had actually spread. Consequently, the situational competence of the language became overvalued and at the same time "upheld" in its place of origin. A generalizing universal is always ethnocentric. This movement, which is centripetal, is the opposite of the elementary, brutal expansion of Anglo-American, which doesn't bother itself with values or worry much about the future of the English language, as long as the sabir obtained in and through this expansion works to maintain actual domination. Imperialism (the thought as well as the reality of empire) does not conceive of anything universal but in every instance is a substitute for it.

We can see another difference in the relationship, whether manifest or latent, of these vehicular languages to the vernacular or composite or subversive languages with which they have been in contact. Attempts have been made to understand why, during European expansion in the Caribbean, only French gave rise to compromise languages—the francophone Creoles—that get away from it and at the same time remain dangerously close. Other languages that spread into these regions permitted only pidgins or subversive practices inscribed within the language itself or distinctive features that only emphasized regional cultural characteristics, without, apparently, calling into question the organic unicity of each of these vehicular languages.* The result of this is that Spanish, for instance, really became the national language of Cubans and Colombians, with no spectacular problems or acknowledged conflicts. This did not happen with French. The language underwent far greater changes when it became Quebecois; it was not able to serve as an unproblematic national language for the states of former French-speaking Africa; nor—because of diglossia—could it "naturally" be the language of inspiration for the people of the Antilles or Réunion.**

Despite these differences in situation, one cannot help but notice that, in varying degrees of complexity, there exist several English, Spanish, or French languages (not counting the Anglo-American sabir that everybody readily uses). Whatever the degree of complexity, the one thing henceforth outmoded is the principle (if not the reality) of a language's intangible unicity. Multiplicity has invaded vehicular languages and is an internal part of them from now on, even when—like Spanish—they seem to resist any centrifugal movement. What does this multiplicity consist of? The implicit renunciation of an arrogant, monolingual separateness and the temptation to participate in worldwide entanglement.

We can deduce three results of this: first, the bolstering of old oral, vernacular, or composite languages, their fixing and

*What I call Creole here (and contrary, perhaps, to the rules) is a language whose lexicon and syntax belong to two heterogeneous linguistic masses: Creole is a compromise. What I call pidgin is a lexical and syntactical reforming within the mass of a single language, with an aggressive will to deformation, which is what distinguishes pidgin from a dialect. Both practices are products of an active creolization.

**What I call diglossia (an idea that made its appearance in linguistics, though linguists say it doesn't work) is the domination of one language over one or several others in the same region.

transcription, will necessarily be subjected to the hazards of this internal complexity that is now part of the system of languages. It would be almost futile and even dangerous to defend these languages from a monolinguistic point of view, because this would enclose them within an ideology and a practice that are already outmoded. Next, any method of learning or translation today has to take into account this internal multiplicity of languages, which goes even further than the old divisions of dialects that were peculiar to each language. Finally, and this observation is how the process operates, the share of opacity allotted to each language, whether vehicular or vernacular, dominating or dominated, is vastly increased by this new multiplicity. The situational competence of each of the languages of our world is overdetermined by the complexity of these relationships. The internal multiplicity of languages here confirms the reality of multilingualism and corresponds to it organically. Our poetics are overwhelmed by it.

It is, therefore, an anachronism, in applying teaching or translation techniques, to teach *the* French language or to translate into *the* French language. It is an epistemological anachronism, by means of which people continue to consider as classic, hence eternal, something that apparently does not "comprehend" opacity or tries to stand in the way of it. Whatever the craven purist may say (and he has neither Étiemble's arguments nor his force of conviction, hunting down sabirs), there are several French languages today, and languages allow us to conceive of their unicity according to a new mode, in which French can no longer be monolingual. If language is given in advance, if it claims to have a mission, it misses out on the adventure and does not *catch on* in the world.

The same is true for those languages that are currently struggling inside the folklore pigeonhole. Through fixation and new methods of transcription they are trying to join into the baroque chorus, the violent and cunningly extended framework of our intertextuality. But because intertextuality is neither fusion nor confusion, if it is to be fruitful and capable of transcendence, the languages that end up involved in it must first have been in charge of their own specificities. Consequently, it is all the more urgent to carefully untangle moments of diglossia. If one is in too much of a hurry to join the concert, there is a risk of mistaking as autonomous participation something that is only some disguised leftover of former alienations. Opacities must be preserved; an appetite for opportune obscurity in translation must be created; and falsely convenient vehicular sabirs must be relentlessly refuted. The framework is not made of transparency; and it is not enough to assert one's right to linguistic difference or, conversely, to interlexicality, to be sure of realizing them.

It would be worthwhile for someone who works with languages to reverse the order of questions and begin his approach by shedding light on the relations of language-culture-situation to the world. That is, by contemplating a poetics. Otherwise, he runs the risk of turning in circles within a code, whose fragile first stirrings he stubbornly insists on legitimizing, to establish the illusion that it is scientific, doing so at the very point in this concert that languages would already have slipped away toward other, fruitful and unpredictable controversies.

# The Black Beach

The beach at Le Diamant on the southern coast of Martinique has a subterranean, cyclical life. During the rainy season, *hivernage,* it shrinks to a corridor of black sand that you would almost think had come from the slopes above, where Mont Pelée branches out into foliage of quelled lava. As if the sea kept alive some underground intercourse with the volcano's hidden fire. And I imagine those murky layers undulating along the sea floor, bringing to our airy regions a convoy of this substance of night and impassive ashes ripened by the harshness of the north.

Then the beach is whipped by a wind not felt on the body; it is a secret wind. High waves come in, lifting close to the shore, they form less than ten meters out, the green of *campêche* trees, and in this short distance they unleash their countless galaxies. Branches of manchineel and seagrape lie about in havoc, writing in the more peaceful sunlight a memoir of the night sea's work. Brown seaweed piled there by the invisible assault buries the line between sand and soil. Uprooted coconut palms have tumbled sideways like stricken bodies. Along their trail, all the way to the rocky mound marking the distant Morne Larcher, one can sense the power of a hurricane one knows will come.

Just as one knows that in *carême,* the dry season, this chaotic grandeur will be carried off, made evanescent by the return of white sand and slack seas. The edge of the sea thus represents the alternation (but one that is illegible) between

121

order and chaos. The established municipalities do their best to manage this constant movement between threatening excess and dreamy fragility.

The movement of the beach, this rhythmic rhetoric of a shore, do not seem to me gratuitous. They weave a circularity that draws me in.

This is where I first saw a ghostly young man go by; his tireless wandering traced a frontier between the land and water as invisible as floodtide at night. I'm not sure what he was called, because he no longer answered to any given name. One morning he started walking and began to pace up and down the shore. He refused to speak and no longer admitted the possibility of any language. His mother became desperate; his friends tried in vain to break down the barrier of total silence. He didn't get angry; he didn't smile; he would move vaguely when a car missed him by a hair or threatened to knock him down. He walked, pulling the belt of his pants up around his waist and wrapping it tighter as his body grew thinner and thinner. It doesn't feel right to have to represent someone so rigorously adrift, so I won't try to describe him. What I would like to show is the nature of this speechlessness. All the languages of the world had come to die here in the quiet, tortured rejection of what was going on all around him in this country: another constant downward drift yet one performed with an anxious satisfaction; the obtrusive sounds of an excitement that is not sure of itself, the pursuit of a happiness that is limited to shaky privileges, the imperceptible numbing effect of quarrels taken to represent a major battle. All this he rejected, casting us out to the edges of his silence.

I made an attempt to communicate with this absence. I respected his stubborn silence, but (frustrated by my inability to make myself "understood" or accepted) wanted nonetheless to establish some system of relation with this walker that was not based on words. Since he went back and forth with the regularity of a metronome in front of the little garden between our house and the beach, one day I called him silently. I didn't exactly know what sign to make—it had to be something neither affected or condescending but also not critical or distant. That time he didn't answer, but the second or third time around (since without being insistent I was insisting) he replied with a sign that was minute, at least to my eyes; for this gesture was perhaps the utmost he was capable of expressing: "I understand what you are attempting to undertake. You are trying to find out why I walk like this— not-here. I accept your trying. But look around and see if it's worth explaining. Are you, yourself, worth my explaining this to you? So, let's leave it at that. We have gone as far as we can together." I was inordinately proud to have gotten this answer.

It was really a minute, imperceptible signal, sort of seesawing his barely lifted hand, and it became (because I adopted it as well) our sign of complicity. It seemed to me that we were perfecting this sign language, adding shades of all the possible meanings that chanced along. So until my departure we shared scraps of the language of gesture that Jean-Jacques Rousseau claimed preceded all spoken language.

I thought of the people struggling within this speck of the world against silence and obliteration. And of how they—in the obstinacy of their venture—have consented to being reduced to sectarianism, stereotyped discourse, zeal, to convoy definitive truths, the appetite for power. And also of what Alain Gontrand has described so well as "our masquerades of temperament." I thought about those people throughout the rest of the world (and the rest, moreover, is what is on the move) who have not had the opportunity to take refuge, as this walker has, in absence—having been forced out by raw poverty, extortion, famines, or massacres. It is paradoxical that so many acts of violence everywhere produce language at its most rudimentary, if not the extinction of words. Is there no valid language for Chaos? Or does Chaos only produce a sort of language that reduces and annihilates? Does its echo recede into a sabir of sabirs at the level of a roar?

The beach, however, has confirmed its volcanic nature. The water now runs along the sea wall of rocks heaped there, a souvenir of former hurricane damage, Beulah or David. The black sand glistens under the foam like peeling skin. The shoreline is cornered, up among coconut palms that now stand in the sea, hailing with their foliage—so perfectly suited—the energy of the deep. We gauge the more and more drastic shrinkage as the winter season strengthens. Then, abruptly, at least for those of us attentive to such changes, the water subsides, daily creating a wider and wider grayish strip. Don't get the idea that this is a tide. But, still, it is on the ebb! The beach, as it broadens, is the precursor of a future *carême*.

It seemed to me that the silent walker accelerated the rhythm of his walks. And that exhilaration also infected the surrounding country. At all costs we wanted to imitate the motion we felt everywhere else, by synthesizing, agitating, and speeding everything up (noise, speech, things to eat and drink, *zouc*, automobiles). Forgetting ourselves any way possible in any kind of speed.

Then, in this circularity I haunt, I turned my efforts toward seeing the beach's backwash into the nearby eddying void as the equivalent of the circling of this man completely withdrawn into his motor forces; tried to relate them, and myself as well, to this rhythm of the world that we consent to without being able to measure or control its course. I thought how everywhere, and in how many different modes, it is the same necessity to fit into the chaotic drive of totality that is at work, despite being subjected to the exaltations or numbing effects of specific existences. I thought about these modes that are just so many commonplaces: the fear, the wasting away, the tortured extinction, the obstinate means of resistance, the naive belief, the famines that go unmentioned, the trepidation, the stubborn determination to learn, the imprisonments, the hopeless struggles, the withdrawal and isolation, the arrogant powers, the blind wealth, the maintenance of the status quo, the numbness, the hidden ideologies, the flaunted ideologies, the crime, the whole mess, the ways of being racist, the slums, the sophisticated techniques, the simple games, the subtle games, the desertions and betrayals, the unshrinking lives, the schools that work, the schools in ruin, the power plots, the prizes for excellence, the children they shoot, the computers, the classrooms with neither paper nor pencils, the exacerbated starvation, the tracking of quarry, the strokes of luck, the ghettos, the assimilations, the immigrations, the Earth's illnesses, the religions, the mind's illnesses, the musics of passion, the rages of what we so simply call libido, the pleasures of our urges and athletic pleasures, and so many other infinite variations of life and death. That these commonplaces, whose quantities are both countless and precise, in fact produced this Roar, in which we could still hear intoned every language in the world. Chaos has no language but gives rise to quantifiable myriads of them. We puzzle out the cycle of their confluences, the tempo of their momentums, the similarities of their diversions.

The beach now undergoes tempestuous change. The sand is the color of confusion, neither dull nor bright, and yet it suits the quality of the atmosphere and wind. The sea is unseasonably foamy: one feels that it will soon subdue the attacks on shoaling rocks. It is haloed by flickering surfaces. As if this reality (the sand, the sea trees, the volcano's conductive water) organized its economy according to a cyclical plan, buttressed by disorder. Those fantastic projects set up every two years or so to save the country crossed my mind: every one of them determined by notions of subjection and inevitably destroyed, swallowed up by personal profit. I wondered whether, in little countries such as ours ("I believe in the future of little countries"), economic prospects (their inspiration) ought not to be more like the beach at Le Diamant: cyclical, changeable, mutating, running through an economy of disorder whose detail would be meticulously calculated but whose comprehensive view would change rapidly depending on different circumstances.

When, in fact, we list unmethodically some of the realms demonstrating every level of economic development in a country like this—the infrastructure and its maintainence, the terms of investment, the budget of the state (what state?), professional training, the search for prospects, energy sources (what sources?), unemployment, the will to create, Social Security coverage, taxes, union dialogue, the internal market, import-export, capital accumulation, the division of the national product (of what nation?)—every single one is in crisis, nonexistent, or impossible; not one has summoned its inspiration from independent political power; furthermore, all are products of structural disorder inherited from colonization, which no adjustment of parity (between the former colony and the former home country) and, moreover, no planning of an ideological order could ever remedy.

That is what we have to shake off. To return to the sources of our cultures and the mobility of their relational content, in order to have a better appreciation of this disorder and to modulate every action according to it. To adapt action to the various possibilities in turn: to the subsistence economy as it existed on the Plantation fringes; to a market economy as the contemporary world imposes it upon us; to a regional economy, in order to reunite with the reality of our Caribbean surroundings; and to a controlled economy whose forms have been suggested by what we have learned from the sciences.

To forsake the single perspective of an economy whose central mechanism is maximum subsidization, that has to be obtained at the whim of an other. Obsession with these subsidies year after year clots thought, paralyzes initiative, and tends to distribute the manna to the most exuberant, neglecting perhaps those who are the most effective.

An economy of disorder, which, I now recall, Marc Guillaume had turned into a completely different theory (*Éloge du désordre*, Gallimard, 1978), but perhaps it is one that would be akin to what Samir Amin said about autocentric economies. Madness! was my first thought. Then—madness!

126

they jeer. But this is madness made up of considerable possibilities of reflection for experts in the matter.

Here acceleration becomes the most important virtue. Not the deliberately forgetful haste prevailing everywhere but an intense acuteness of thought, quick to change its heading. The capability of varying speed and direction at any moment, without, however, changing its nature, its intention, or its will, might be perhaps the optimal principle for such an economic system. Course changes would be dependent on a harsh analysis of reality. As for steadfastness of intention and will, this we would forge as we come to know our cultures.

This acceleration and speed race across the Earth. "And yet, it does turn!" Galileo's aside did not simply determine a new order in our knowledge of the stars; it prophesied the circularity of languages, the convergent speed of cultures, the autonomy (in relation to any dogma) of the resultant energy.

But, while I was wandering like this, a silence as dizzying as speed and disorder gradually rose from the uproar of the sea.

The voiceless man who walks keeps on carting his black sand from a distant volcano known only to himself, to the beaches he pretends to share with us. How can he run faster when he is growing so desperately thin? One of us whispers: "He goes faster and faster because if he stops, if he slows down—he will fall."

We are not going any faster, we are all hurtling onward— for fear of falling.

IV

# THEORIES

*Theory is absence, obscure and propitious*

# RELATION

*The repercussions of cultures, whether in symbiosis or in
conflict—in a polka, we might say, or in a* laghia—*in
domination or liberation, opening before us an unknown
forever both near and deferred, their lines of force occasionally
divined, only to vanish instantly. Leaving us to imagine their
interaction and shape it at the same time: to dream or to act.*

*The deconstruction of any ideal relationship one might
claim to define in this interaction, out of which ghouls
of totalitarian thinking might suddenly reemerge.*

*The position of each part within this whole: that is, the
acknowledged validity of each specific Plantation yet at the
same time the urgent need to understand the hidden order of
the whole—so as to wander there without becoming lost.*

*The thing recused in every generalization of an absolute, even
and especially some absolute secreted within this imaginary
construct of Relation: that is, the possibility for each one at
every moment to be both solidary and solitary there.*

# The Relative and Chaos

We were circling around the thought of Chaos, sensing that the way Chaos itself goes around is the opposite of what is ordinarily understood by "chaotic" and that it opens onto a new phenomenon: Relation, or totality in evolution, whose order is continually in flux and whose disorder one can imagine forever.

There is a revealing correspondence between the philosophies secreted by the sciences in the West and the conceptions commonly held about or imposed upon cultures and their relations. During the period when positivism was triumphant, culture (and not yet cultures) was conceived of as monolithic, culture existing wherever the refinements of civilization have led to humanism.* When conceived of in this manner, culture is presented as purely abstract, the very essence of this movement toward an ideal. Those who attain it are responsible for this evolution and its pilots. They teach the rest of the world. Montaigne's relativism is forgotten, shoved through a trapdoor and stifled for more than three centuries. It required the illustration of the notion of the relative in the scientific theory of Relativity for an awareness of the relativism of cultures to prevail.[1]

What we commonly grasp of Einsteinian thought is this

*Positivism and humanism have in common the fact that both end up imposing the reality of an "ideal object" that they have initially defined as value.

simple connection between Relativity and the principle of the relative. All the rest lies in ambush within the bastion of theorems. Substituting or compensating for its lack of direct access to what Einstein said, the public has mythologized the scientist. This mythmaking is a sign of the extent to which the relative is powerfully present for us. To the point at which the formula $E = mc^2$ has become a common place (or common-place)[2] that we use advisedly, that is for its symbolic freight, without being sure we really appreciate its content.

What part of this theory do we retain concerning the subject at hand, when we are not limited by our infirmities as nonspecialists? That there is no thought of the absolute but also that the Relation of uncertainty postulated by Heisenberg is not perhaps the basis for an irreversible probabilism. (Are "primary" particles subjected to chance?) For Einstein Relativity is not purely relative. The universe has a "sense" that is neither chance nor necessity: a geometer god (the same as Newton's), in any case a "powerful and mysterious reason"—and not, therefore, a malicious spirit, as in Descartes—provides us with a riddle to decipher. This puzzle (something to be divined through intuition and verified through experimentation) "guarantees" the interactive dynamics of the universe and of our knowledge of it.

Experimental thought has its basis in this interaction and "guarantees" in turn that the puzzle will not be taken into realms of the impossible (something will always be there to grasp) nor into realms of the absolute (something will always remain to be grasped).

The totality within which Relativity is exerted and to which it is applied, through the workings of the mind, is not totalitarian, therefore: not imposed a priori, not fixed as an absolute. And, consequently, for the mind, it is neither a restrictive dogmatism nor the skepticism of probabilist thought.

Consent to cultural relativism ("each human culture has value in its own milieu, becoming equivalent to every other in the ensemble") accompanied the spreading awareness of, and adherence or at least habituation to, the idea of Relativity.

This cultural relativism has not always come without a tinge of essentialism, which has colored even the concepts that contributed to challenging the domination of conquering cultures. The idea of *one* Africa, conceived of as undivided, and the theory of Negritude (among French speakers) are two examples of this frequently debated for that very reason.

Furthermore, this relativism in turn has been regarded as falling into the category of a "golden mean." Here diversity exists among cultures but does not prevent the formation of hierarchies among civilizations. Or, at the very least, an ascent (regular or intermittent) toward the transparency of a world—or model— that is universal. And, consequently, for the mind there is neither totalitarian ethnocentrism nor the anarchy of a tabula rasa. Montaigne's invaluable idea was adapted to suit the tendentious drone of this new version of humanism. This form of relativism has no pertinence to the relative.

Just as Relativity in the end postulated a Harmony to the universe, cultural relativism (Relativity's timid and faltering reflection) viewed and organized the world through a global transparency that was, in the last analysis, reductive. This cultural "Society of Nations" could not withstand the maelstrom.

But the dogmatic feeling of superiority and the clever maneuvers of false relativism were succeeded by an elegant disenchantment, the acute sense of the futility of it all. If everything in this maelstrom was equal in fact to everything else, if the realization of an Earth—totality opened onto chaos—what was the use? Pervading what should have been an exhilarating arrival at totality was a flavor of declining empire, reinforced, perhaps, after World War II by the antagonistic presence of the two Roman empires of our time, the United States and the Soviet Union. Both were driven by the same naive belief, frequently confirmed by reality, in their preeminence over other populations. And you might imagine each of these powers, which, having plentiful wealth, did not have to torment themselves so, going around muttering to themselves, "Tonight Lucullus will be eating at Lucullus's table."

Meanwhile, poor nations, by their very eruption, had made it possible for new ideas to be born: ideas of otherness, of difference, of minority rights, of the rights of peoples. These ideas, however, seemed only to dust the surface of the swirling magma. It was not clear how anyone could conceive of the global dereliction of humanities meeting and confronting one another in the spaces and times of the planet.

Then, bit by bit, an idea came together from scientific intuitions: it was possible to study Chaos without succumbing to a vertigo of disillusion over its endless transformations.

Let us venture two of the directions in which the strengths of science either operate or become exasperated.

First, there is the directly technological application, which tends to reactivate a "projective linearity" and sets things up, if not for getting to "the bottom" of the matter (possibly something it will never achieve), at least for discovery or conquest, which are one and the same, of the galactic spaces. Technological thought is clear about the fact that it will never exhaust the yield of the universe but doesn't let this scare it off. On the contrary, it is stymied by the mystery of the infinitely small (of the "prime element"), dreading the discovery there of an infinitely receding limit.

The Unified Field Theory constructed by Einstein attempted to bridge these two dimensions of the universe and define its undifferentiated unity. But, for the time being, "dominant" scientific thought has apparently renounced either supporting or delving into this theory. It seems, rather, to have returned to the comfortable empiricism that provides immense technological power, having decided to devote itself principally to "exploration," and preferably in the realm of the infinitely large.

This tendency, morever, has become increasingly based on

attempts to imagine or to prove a "creation of the world" (the Big Bang), which has always been the "basis" of the scientific project. The old obsession with filiation carves out a new adornment for itself. Linearity ties in. The idea of God is there. And the notion of legitimacy reemerges. A science of conquerors who scorn or fear limits; a science of conquest.

The other direction, which is not one, distances itself entirely from the thought of conquest; it is an experimental meditation (a follow-through) of the process of relation, at work in reality, among the elements (whether primary or not) that weave its combinations. A science of inquiry. This "orientation" then leads to following through whatever is dynamic, the relational, the chaotic—anything fluid and various and moreover uncertain (that is, ungraspable) yet fundamental in every instance and quite likely full of instances of invariance.

It is true that each of these two tendencies relays and reinforces each other. But the first perpetuates an arrowlike projection, whereas the second, perhaps, recreates the processes of circular nomadism. It is also true that dispossessed regions, countries in the throes of absolute poverty, are isolated from participation. But, though they don't "count" for conquering science (except as a ruthless reserve of primary material), their presence constitutes another material, the one covered by inquiring science. The subject matter of this science is *chaos-monde,* one of the modes of Chaos.

This is not a passive participation. Passivity plays no part in Relation. Every time an individual or community attempts to define its place in it, even if this place is disputed, it helps blow the usual way of thinking off course, driving out the now weary rules of former classicisms, making new "follow-throughs" to *chaos-monde* possible.

The science of Chaos renounces linearity's potent grip and, in this expanse/extension, conceives of indeterminacy as a fact that can be analyzed and accident as measurable. By rediscovering the abysses of art or the interplay of various aesthetics, scientific knowledge thus develops one of the ways poetics is expressed, reconnecting with poetry's earlier ambition to establish itself as knowledge.

One can see why philosophies issuing from different "stages" of science have driven successively "established" ideas of cultures and their entanglements. It is because scientific ideas always presuppose generalization (unconsciously influenced by the metaphysics from which they freed themselves) and are suspicious of it in each instance (as every poetics in the world inspires us to be). They have finally been able to understand generalization from the angle of generality, abandoning filiation's linearity for the surplus of expansiveness. This is how the evolution of cultures works.

In expanse/extension the forms of *chaos-monde* (the immeasurable intermixing of cultures) are unforeseeable and foretellable. We have not yet begun to calculate their consequences: the passive adoptions, irrevocable rejections, naive beliefs, parallel lives, and the many forms of confrontation or consent, the many syntheses, surpassings, or returns, the many sudden outbursts of invention, born of impacts and breaking what has produced them, which compose the fluid, turbulent, stubborn, and possibly organized matter of our common destiny.

Is it meaningful, pathetic, or ridiculous that Chinese students have been massacred in front of a cardboard reproduction of the Statue of Liberty? Or that, in a Romanian house, hated portraits of Ceaușescu have been replaced by photographs cut from magazines of characters in the television series "Dallas"? Simply to ask the question is to imagine the unimaginable turbulence of Relation.

Yes, we are just barely beginning to conceive of this immense friction. The more it works in favor of an oppressive order, the more it calls forth disorder as well. The more it produces exclusion, the more it generates attraction. It standardizes—but at every node of Relation we will find callouses of resistance. Relation is learning more and more to go beyond judgments into the unexpected dark of art's upsurgings. Its beauty springs from the stable and the unstable, from the deviance of many particular poetics and the clairvoyance of a relational poetics. The more things it standardizes into a state of lethargy, the more rebellious consciousness it arouses.

We will not gain access to this turbulence through the same means employed by theoreticians and students of Chaos. We do not have at our disposal computers capable of following the flow of cultures, the poetic nodes, the dynamics of languages, the phases of cultures in confrontation. Should we hope that our imaginary construct of Relation might someday be "confirmed" in formulas we can read on the monitor screen? Can accident, which is the joy of poetics, be tamed through circuits? Might it be possible to relate the turbulences of *chaos-monde* in this way (in and through analysis by instruments) to the turbulences of Chaos? Then what would be the consequences of such an intrusion?

Every "virus" (every accident), according to Jacques Coursil, is injected into a computer system; but it would also be possible for it to have been secreted by the system itself. In this case it would be proof that the system "thinks," that, in short, accident is part of its nature. This outcome would also be invaluable for safeguarding freedoms, the guarantee that no Law could ever be founded on such a system. What's more, taking a wild tack with this hypothesis, the virus would manifest the fractal nature of the system; it would be the sign of the intrusion of Chaos, the irremediable indicator, that is, of the asynchronous nature of the system. This is how one might imagine this other unimaginable event: the computer, the privileged instrument for the analysis of Chaos, would be invaded and inhabited by the latter. Chaos, turning back around upon itself, would shut the doors. It would be God. (At least, if no one invented other instruments of investigation that could not be contaminated by their object.) The stubborn determination of analytic thought makes it possible to continue infinitely this perspective of deferral. Really, however, it is only the human imaginary that cannot be contaminated by its objects. Because it alone diversifies them infinitely yet brings them back, nonetheless, to a full burst of unity. The highest point of knowledge is always a poetics.

# Distancing, Determining

Contemporary violence is the response societies make to the immediacy of contacts and is exacerbated by the brutality of the flash agents of Communication.[1] It is not all that easy to forego the comfortable expanses of time formerly allowing changes to occur imperceptibly. In cities this speed becomes concentrated, and the response explodes. These same mechanisms are at work both in cultures of intervention and in emerging cultures: New York or Lagos.* In the shantytowns and ghettos of even the smallest cities the same gears engage: the violence of poverty and mud but also an unconscious and desperate rage at not "grasping" [*com-prendre*] the chaos of the world. Those who dominate benefit from the chaos; those who are oppressed are exasperated by it.

This speeding up of relationships has repercussions on how the full-sense of identity is understood. The latter is no longer linked, except in an occasionally anachronistic or more often lethal manner, to the sacred mystery of the root. It depends on how a society participates in global relation, registers its speed, and controls its conveyance or doesn't. Identity is no longer just permanence; it is a capacity for variation, yes, a variable—either under control or wildly fluctuating.

The old idea of identity as root, whenever it proves hard to

*The cultures that I call "emerging" are those that do not have at their disposal the institutionalized—nor, for that matter, improvised—means of speaking up in the planetary flow of Communication.

141

define or impossible to maintain, leads inexorably to the refuges of generalization provided by the universal as value. This is how the elite populations in southern countries have usually reacted when choosing to renounce their own difficult definition. A generalizing universal reassures them. Identity as a system of relation, as an aptitude for "giving-on-and-with" [*donner-avec*], is, in contrast, a form of violence that challenges the generalizing universal and necessitates even more stringent demands for specificity. But it is hard to keep in balance.* Why is there this paradox in Relation? Why the necessity to approach the specificities of communities as closely as possible? To cut down on the danger of being bogged down, diluted, or "arrested" in undifferentiated conglomerations.

But, in any case, the speed with which geocultural entities, aggregates formed through encounters and kinships, change in the world is relative. For example, there is a real situational community among the creolizing cultures of the Caribbean and those of the Indian Ocean (in Réunion or Seychelles). However, there is nothing to say that accelerated evolution will not soon entail equally powerful and decisive encounters between the Caribbean region and Brazil, or among the smaller Antillean islands (both French- and English-speaking), that will lead to the formation of new zones of relational community. It would not be possible to base ontological thinking on the existence of entities such as these, whose very nature is to vary tremendously within Relation. This variation is, on the contrary, evidence that ontological thought no longer "functions," no longer provides a founding certainty that is stock-still, once and for all, in a restrictive territory.

In such an evolution we are justified in maintaining the following principle: "Relation exists, especially as the particulars that are its interdependent constituent have first freed themselves from any approximation of dependency."

*There is a growing tendency in Western aesthetic theories, from ethnopoetics to geopoetics to cosmopoetics, to make some claim of going beyond notions or dimensions of identity.

Gradually, premonitions of the interdependence at work in the world today have replaced the ideologies of national independence that drove the struggles for decolonization. But the absolute presupposition of this interdependence is that instances of independence will be defined as closely as possible and actually won or sustained. Because it is only beneficial to all (it only stops being a pretext or ruse) at the point at which it governs the distancings that are determinant.

One of the most dramatic consequences of interdependence concerns the hazards of emigration. When identity is determined by a root, the emigrant is condemned (especially in the second generation) to being split and flattened. Usually an outcast in the place he has newly set anchor, he is forced into impossible attempts to reconcile his former and his present belonging.

Despite their French citizenship, most of the Antilleans who live in France, participating in the widespread movement of emigration into this country (North Africans, Portuguese, Senegalese, etc.), have not been spared this condition. It is through a rather impressive turnabout in history, in Martinique, that its leaders are now speaking up to suggest that it would not, after all, be such a bad thing to participate in a dignified manner in this citizenship.

Summarizing what we know concerning the varieties of identity, we arrive at the following:

*Root identity*
—is founded in the distant past in a vision, a myth of the creation of the world;
—is sanctified by the hidden violence of a filiation that strictly follows from this founding episode;
—is ratified by a claim to legitimacy that allows a community to proclaim its entitlement to the possession of a land, which thus becomes a territory;
—is preserved by being projected onto other territories,

making their conquest legitimate—and through the project of a discursive knowledge.

Root identity therefore rooted the thought of self and of territory and set in motion the thought of the other and of voyage.

*Relation identity*
- —is linked not to a creation of the world but to the conscious and contradictory experience of contacts among cultures;
- —is produced in the chaotic network of Relation and not in the hidden violence of filiation;
- —does not devise any legitimacy as its guarantee of entitlement, but circulates, newly extended;
- —does not think of a land as a territory from which to project toward other territories but as a place where one gives-on-and-with rather than grasps.

Relation identity exults the thought of errantry and of totality.

The shock of relating, hence, has repercussions on several levels. When secular cultures come into contact through their intolerances, the ensuing violence triggers mutual exclusions that are of a sacred nature and for which any future reconciliation is hard to foresee. When a culture that is expressly composite, such as the culture of Martinique, is touched by another (French) that "entered into" its composition and continues to determine it, not radically but through the erosion of assimilation, the violence of reaction is intermittent and unsure of itself. For the Martinican it has no solid rootstock in any sacred territory or filiation. This, indeed, is a case in which specificity is a strict requirement and must be defined as closely as possible. For this composite culture is fragile in the extreme, wearing down through contact with a masked colonization.

Consequently, wouldn't it be best just to go along with it? Wouldn't it be a viable solution to embellish the alienation, to endure while comfortably receiving state assistance, with all the obvious guarantees implied in such a decision? This is what the technocratic elite, created for the management of decoy positions, have to talk themselves into before they convince the people of Martinique. Their task is all the less difficult since they use it to give themselves airs of conciliation, of cooperative humanism, of a realism anxious to make concrete improvements in circumstances. Not counting the pleasures of permissive consumption. Not counting the actual advantages of a special position, in which public funds (from France or Europe) serve to satisfy a rather large number of people (to the benefit, however, of French or European companies that are more and more visible in the country or castes of *békés* converted from former planters into a tertiary sector and thus won over to the ideas of this elite) and serve to foster the hopes of an even greater number.*

And it is true that in a context of this sort one spares oneself both the sacred violence, which is boundless, and the violence of absolute destitution, which is spreading with such lightning speed over half the planet. What remains here is only the suppressed and intermittent violence of a community convulsively demonstrating its sense of disquiet. What sense of disquiet? The one that comes from having to consume the world without participating in it, without even the least idea of it, without being able to offer it anything other than a vague homily to a generalizing universal. Privileged disquiet.

Traumatic reaction is not, however, the only form of resistance in Martinique. In a nonatavistic society of this sort three rallying points have grown in strength: relationship with the natural surroundings, the Caribbean; defense of the

*This year (1990) Martinique, which is an underdeveloped country with 40 percent unemployment, consumed 1.3 tons of Iranian caviar (imported from France) and forty million francs' worth of champagne; there are 173,000 cars registered for its 320,000 inhabitants. As the television newscaster, in a felicitous commentary on these figures, said, "We'll do better next year!"

people's language, Creole; protection of the land, by mobilizing everyone. Three modes of existence that challenge the establishment (three cultural reflexes that are not without ambiguity themselves), that do not link, however, the severe demand for specificity to the intolerance of a root but, rather, to an ecological vision of Relation.

Ecology, going above and beyond its concerns with what we call the environment, seems to us to represent mankind's drive to extend to the planet Earth the former sacred thought of Territory. Thus, it has a double orientation: either it can be conceived of as a by-product of this sacred and in this case be experienced as mysticism, or else this extending thought will bear the germ of criticism of territorial thought (of its sacredness and exclusiveness), so that ecology will then act as politics.

The politics of ecology has implications for populations that are decimated or threatened with disappearance as a people. For, far from consenting to sacred intolerance, it is a driving force for the relational interdependence of all lands, of the whole Earth. It is this very interdependence that forms the basis for entitlement. Other factors become null and void.

Concerning the Antilles, for example, there is a lot of discussion concerning the legitimacy of land "possession." According to the mysterious laws of rootedness (of filiation), the only "possessors" of the Archipelago would be the Caribs or their predecessors, who have been exterminated. The restrictive force of the sacred always tends to seek out the first occupants of a territory (those closest to an original "creation"). So, in the Caribbean would this be Caribs and Arawaks or other older and, consequently, more legitimate and "determining" populations? The massacre of the Indians, uprooting the sacred, has already invalidated this futile search. Once that had happened, Antillean soil could not become a territory but, rather, a rhizomed land. Indeed, Martinican soil does not belong as a rooted absolute either to the

146

descendants of deported Africans or to the *békés* or to the Hindus or to the mulattoes. But the consequences of European expansion (extermination of the Pre-Columbians, importation of new populations) is precisely what forms the basis for a new relationship with the land: not the absolute ontological possession regarded as sacred but the complicity of relation. Those who have endured the land's constraint, who are perhaps mistrustful of it, who have perhaps attempted to escape it to forget their slavery, have also begun to foster these new connections with it, in which the sacred intolerance of the root, with its sectarian exclusiveness, has no longer any share.

Ecological mysticism relies on this intolerance. A reactionary, that is to say infertile, way of thinking about the Earth, it would almost be akin to the "return to the land" championed by Pétain, whose only instinct was to reactivate the forces of tradition and abdication while at the same time appealing to a withdrawal reflex.

In Western countries these two ecological options (political and mystical) come together in action. Still, one cannot ignore the differences that drive them. Not acknowledging these differences in our countries predisposes us in favor of mimetic practices that are either quite simply imported because of the pressures of Western opinion or else the baggage of standardized fashion, such as jogging and hiking.

We end up every time with the following axiom—one not given in advance: Pronouncing one's specificity is not enough if one is to escape the lethal, indistinct confusion of assimilations; this specificity still has to be put into action before consenting to any outcome.

But the axiom, though not a priori, is unbending when applied. A perilous equilibrium exists between self-knowledge and another's practice. If we are to renounce intolerances, why hold out against outright consent? And, if we are to follow our freedom to its "logical consequences," why not have the right to confirm it in a radical negation of the Other?

147

These dilemmas have their own particular areas of application to govern. Such as the need for poor countries to exercise self-sufficiency that is economically and physically sustaining. Such as the definition of how forms of independence are experienced or hoped for. Such as the putting into practice of ethnotechnology as an instrument of self-sufficiency. Never have obligations been so chancy in reality.

To oppose the disturbing affective standardization of peoples, whose affect has been diverted by the processes and products of international exchange, either consented to or imposed, it is necessary to renew the visions and aesthetics of relating to the earth.

But, since sensibilities have already been diverted widely by these processes of exchange, it will not be easy to get anyone to replace products bearing an intense relational charge, such as Coca-Cola, wheat bread, or dairy butter with yams, breadfruit or a revived production of *madou, mabi* or any other "local" products. All the more since products of this sort, whose excellence depends on their fragility, do not tend to keep well, which is one of the secrets of large-scale commerce. Standardization of taste is "managed" by the industrial powers.

There are plenty of native Martinicans who will confess that when they were children they used to hate breadfruit (a staple vegetable and, therefore, intimately associated with the idea of poverty and the reality of destitution). Then the reverse has become true with age, especially for those who have lived for a long time away from the island—they have acquired a lasting taste for it. Any survey taken would show the same to be true today for most of the children in Martinique. With a fierce "tchip!" of the lips, children reject even the thought of breadfruit and relish the idea of dried sausage. In countries in which imports reign, childhood is the first deportee.

I made note of someone who, claiming to criticize novelists from Martinique whose vision of reality is expressed in the poetics of a language irrigated by Creole, spoke disdainfully of "*dachinisme*" (from the word *dachine* [dasheen], or Chinese cabbage, another local vegetable). Thus, the same negativity is used to punish any production that does not consent to international standardization or conform to the generalizing universal.

In rich nations, in which imports are balanced with more or less difficulty by exports and in which, consequently, foreign goods offered for consumption are exchanged more or less indirectly against local production, it is easier to maintain equilibrium between the levels. The international product has a less severe impact on sensibilities; "desire" for it is not so implacable.

In poor countries any appeal for self-sufficiency grounded solely in economics and good sense is doomed to failure. Good sense is of no consequence in the tangle of world Relation. Sensibilities have become so profoundly contaminated, in most cases, and the habit of material comfort is so well established, even in the midst of the greatest poverty, that political dictates or proclamations are inadequate remedies. Here, as elsewhere, one must figure out how much we have to consent to the planetary evolution toward standardization of consumer products (the present course in Martinique, with French products widely imported) and how much we should push for invention and a new sensibility in association with "national" products.

This is where the imagination and expression of an aesthetics of the earth—freed from quaint naïveté, to rhizome instead throughout our cultures' understanding—become indispensable.

It is certainly true that we do not work the land, are no longer the country people we used to be, with our same old instinctive patience. Too many international parameters come into this relationship. A man involved in agriculture is inevitably a man involved in culture: he can no longer produce innocently.

Daily we hear about how occupations connected with the land are among the sorriest that exist. The farmer's traditional solitude has become exacerbated by the embarrassed thought that his work is anachronistic, in developed countries, or pathetic, in poor countries. In the former he struggles against productivity, taxes, markets, and surplus; in the latter against dust, the lack of tools, epidemics, and shortages. Both here and there the display of technological wealth overwhelms him. It would be obnoxious to indulge in idiotic praise of the peasantry when it is going downhill this way everywhere. Will it die, or will it be transformed into a reserve labor force for advanced techniques?

It is said—a commonplace—that the future of humanity is at stake, unless, before extinction, such techniques make possible the massive production of artificial foods that would take care of the richest. Picture an uncultivated land when the factories producing synthetics have provided enough for the stomachs of the chosen few. It would only be used for leisure, for a kind of Voyage in which seeking and knowledge would have no place at all. It would become scenery. That is what would happen to our countries, since it is entirely possible that the aforesaid factories would never be located in them (unless they are really responsible for producing too much waste). We would inhabit Museums of Natural Non-History. Reactivating an aesthetics of the earth will perhaps help differ this nightmare, air-conditioned or not.

This trend toward international standardization of consumption will not be reversed unless we make drastic changes in the diverse sensibilities of communities by putting forward the prospect—or at least the possibility—of this revived aesthetic connection with the earth.

How can such a poetics be resuscitated, when its mind-set drifts between the obsolete mysticism that we noted and the mockery of production that is emerging everywhere? An aesthetics of the earth seems, as always, anachronistic or naive: reactionary or sterile.

But we must get beyond this seemingly impossible task. If we don't, all the prestige (and denaturation) felt in internationally standardized consumption will triumph permanently over the pleasure of consuming one's own product. The problem is that these denaturations create imbalance and dry things up. Understood in its full-sense, passion for the land where one lives is a start, an action we must endlessly risk.

An aesthetics of the earth? In the half-starved dust of Africas? In the mud of flooded Asias? In epidemics, masked forms of exploitation, flies buzz-bombing the skeleton skins of children? In the frozen silence of the Andes? In the rains uprooting *favelas* and shantytowns? In the scrub and scree of Bantu lands? In flowers encircling necks and ukuleles? In mud huts crowning goldmines? In city sewers? In haggard aboriginal wind? In red-light districts? In drunken indiscriminate consumption? In the noose? The cabin? Night with no candle?

Yes. But an aesthetics of disruption and intrusion. Finding the fever of passion for the ideas of "environment" (which I call surroundings) and "ecology," both apparently such futile notions in these landscapes of desolation. Imagining the idea of love of the earth—so ridiculously inadequate or else frequently the basis for such sectarian intolerance—with all the strength of charcoal fires or sweet syrup.

Aesthetics of rupture and connection.

Because that is the crux of it, and almost everything is said in pointing out that under no circumstances could it ever be a question of transforming land into territory again. Territory is the basis for conquest. Territory requires that filiation be planted and legitimated. Territory is defined by its limits, and they must be expanded. A land henceforth has no limits. That is the reason it is worth defending against every form of alienation.

Aesthetics of a variable continuum, of an invariant discontinuum.

Self-sufficiency can be worked out. With the sole condition that it not end up in the exclusivity of territory. A necessary condition but not enough to incite the radicalities capable of saving us from ambiguity, rallied together within a landscape—reforming our taste, without our having to force ourselves into it.

Thus, within the pitiless panorama of the worldwide commercial market, we debate our problems. No matter where you are or what government brings you together into a community, the forces of this market are going to find you. If there is profit to be made, they will deal with you. These are not vague forces that you might accommodate out of politeness; these are hidden forces of inexorable logic that must be answered with the total logic of your behavior. For example, one could not accept state assistance and at the same time pretend to oppose it. You must choose your bearing. And, to get back to the question raised earlier, simply consenting would not be worth it, in any case. Contradiction would knot the community (which ceases to be one) with impossibilities, profoundly destabilizing it. The entire country would become a Plantation, believing it operates with freedom of decision but, in fact, being outer directed. The exchange of goods (in this case in Martinique: the exchange of imported public money against exported private profit) is the rule. Bustling commerce only confirms the fragmentation and opposition to change. Minds get used up in this superficial comfort, which has cost them an unconscious, enervating braining.

This is the dilemma to be resolved. We have learned that peremptory declarations, grounded in the old Manichaeanism of liberation, are of no use here, because they only contribute to reinforcing a stereotypical language with no hold in reality. These are all liabilities whose dialectics must first be either realized or bypassed.

Thinking, for example, that ethnotechnology would save us from excessive importation, protect the vivid physical quality of the country, find an equilibrium for our drive to consume, and cement links among all the individuals concerned with producing and creating amounts to saying that we would return to a pretechnical, artisan level, elevated to the rank of a system, leaving it to others to take care of providing us with the spin-off from their dizzying experiments, making us admire from afar the achievements of their science, and renting us (but under what conditions) the fruits of their industry. Have something to exchange that isn't just sand and coconut trees but, instead, the result of our creative activity. Integrate what we have, even if it is sea and sun, with the adventure of a culture that is ours to share and for which we take responsibility.

There is no value to practicing self-sufficiency, or consenting to interdependance, or mastering ethnotechnology, unless these processes constitute both distancings from and accord with (and in relation to) their referent: the multiform elsewhere always set forth as a monolithic necessity in any country that is dominated.

We struggle against our problems, without knowing that throughout the world they are widespread. There is no place that does not have its elsewhere. No place where this is not an essential dilemma. No place where it is not necessary to come as close as possible to figuring out this dialectic of interdependencies or this difficult necessity for ethnotechniques.

The massive and diffracted confluence of cultures thus makes every distancing (from a suggested or imposed prenorm) be determinant but also makes every (self-)determination be a generative distancing.

Now let us try to summarize the things we don't yet know, the things we have no current means of knowing, concerning all the singularities, all the trajectories, all the histories, all the forms of denaturation, and all the syntheses that are at work or that have resulted from our confluences. How have cultures—Chinese or Basque, Indian or Inuit, Polynesian or Alpine—made their way to us, and how have we reached them? What remains to us of all the vanished cultures, collapsed or exterminated, and in what form? What is our experience, even now, of the pressure of dominant cultures? Through what fantastic accumulations of how many existences, both individual and collective? Let us try to calculate the result of all that. We will be incapable of doing so. Our experience of this confluence will forever be only one part of its totality.

No matter how many studies and references we accumulate (though it is our profession to carry out such things), we will never reach the end of such a volume; knowing this in advance makes it possible for us to dwell there. Not knowing this totality is not a weakness. Not wanting to know it certainly is. Consequently, we imagine it through a poetics: this imaginary realm provides the full-sense of all these always decisive differentiations. A lack of this poetics, its absence or its negation, would constitute a failing.*

Similarly, thought of the Other is sterile without the other of Thought.

Thought of the Other is the moral generosity disposing me to accept the principle of alterity, to conceive of the world as not simple and straightforward, with only one truth—mine. But thought of the Other can dwell within me without making me alter course, without "prizing me open," without changing me within myself. An ethical principle, it is enough that I not violate it.

The other of Thought is precisely this altering. Then I have to act. That is the moment I change my thought, without renouncing its contribution. I change, and I exchange.

---

*I see the extent to which this imaginary appears to me to have a certain form in space: I spoke of circularity (imitating, perhaps, those curvatures of space-time that Einstein invented) and of volume, the spherical nature of concepts, of various poetics and the realities of the *chaos-monde,* all of which reconstitutes (for me) the image of the mother planet, an Earth that would be primordial. But mothering is excluded from this symbolic system—at least, I believe that it is. As well as the idea (so dear to Aristotle and Ptolemy) of a perfection in circularity.

This is an aesthetics of turbulence whose corresponding ethics is not provided in advance.

If, thus, we allow that an aesthetics is an art of conceiving, imagining, and acting, the other of Thought is the aesthetics implemented by me and by you to join the dynamics to which we are to contribute. This is the part fallen to me in an aesthetics of chaos, the work I am to undertake, the road I am to travel. Thought of the Other is occasionally presupposed by dominant populations, but with an utterly sovereign power, or proposed until it hurts by those under them, who set themselves free. The other of Thought is always set in motion by its confluences as a whole, in which each is changed by and changes the other.

Common sense tells us that the world through which we move is so profoundly disturbed (most would call it crazy) and has such direct repercussions on each one of us that some are obliged to exist in absolute misery and others in a sort of generalized suspension. We line one day up after the other, day after day, as if the world did not exist, though daily it seeks us out with such violence. Yes, we act as if. For if we stopped to think about it really we would let everything go. A commonplace—one I have heard so often repeated.

To suspend the suspense we have recourse to this imaginary construct of totality, by means of which we transmute for ourselves this mad state of the world into a chaos that we are able to contemplate. An imaginary rekindled by the other of Thought. A distancing in relation to the predetermined or imposed norm but also prehaps in relation to the norms or beliefs that we have passively inherited. How can we put this distancing into practice if we have not fully mastered beforehand the things that are ours or part of us? Dependencies are infirmities of Relation, obstacles to the hard work of its entanglement. Independencies, for the same reasons, despite being uncomfortable or precarious, are always worth something.

The suffering of human cultures does not confine us permanently within a mute actuality, mere presence grievously closed. Sometimes this suffering authorizes an absence that constitutes release, soaring over: thought rising from the prisms of poverty, unfurling its own opaque violence, that gives-on-and-with every violence of contact between cultures. The most peaceful thought is, thus, in its turn a violence, when it imagines the risky processes of Relation yet nonetheless avoids the always comfortable trap of generalization. This antiviolence violence is no trivial thing; it is opening and creation. It adds a full-sense to the operative violence of those on the margins, the rebels, the deviants, all specialists in distancing.

The marginal and the deviant sense in advance the shock of cultures; they live its future excess. The rebel paves the way for such a shock, or at least its legibility, by refusing to be cramped by any tradition at all, even when the force of his rebellion comes from the defense of a tradition that is ridiculed or oppressed by another tradition that simply has more powerful means of action. The rebel defends his right to do his own surpassing; the lives of marginal and deviant persons take this right to extremes.

We have not yet begun to imagine or figure out the results of all the distancings that are determinant. They have emerged from everywhere, bearing every tradition and the surpassing of them all, in a confluence that does away with trajectories (itineraries), all the while realizing them in the end.

Though the cultural contacts of the moment are terrifyingly "immediate," another vast expanse of time looms before us, nonetheless: it is what will be necessary to counterbalance specific situations, to defuse oppressions, to assemble the poetics. This time to come seems as infinite as galactic spaces.

Meanwhile, contemporary violence is one of the logics—organic—of the turbulence of the *chaos-monde*. This violence is what instinctively opposes any thought intending to make this chaos monolithic, grasping it to control it.

Distancings are necessary to Relation and depend on it: like the coexistence of sea olive and manchineel.

# That That

## 1

The world's poetic force (its energy), kept alive within us, fastens itself by fleeting, delicate shivers, onto the rambling prescience of poetry in the depths of our being. The active violence in reality distracts us from knowing it. Our obligation to "grasp" violence, and often fight it, estranges us from such live intensity, as it also freezes the shiver and disrupts prescience. But this force never runs dry because it is its own turbulence.* Poetry—thus, nonetheless, totality gathering strength—is driven by another poetic dimension that we all divine or babble within ourselves. It could well be that poetry is basically and mainly defined in this relationship of itself to nothing other than itself, of density to volatility, or the whole to the individual.

This world force does not direct any line of force but infinitely reveals them. Like a landscape impossible to epitomize. It forces us to imagine it even while we stand there neutral and passive.

Borne along by this force or raging to control it—not yet having consented to the greatness that would come from par-

*The idea of this energy makes for a good joke: "the Force" is the leitmotiv for a very famous metaphysical/western movie sequence.

taking of it—it will be a long time before we finally recognize it as the newness of the world not setting itself up as anything new.

The expression of this force and its way of being is what we call Relation: what the world makes and expresses of itself.


2


When we ask the question of what is brought into play by Relation, we arrive at that-there that cannot be split up into original elements. We are scarcely at liberty to approach the complete interaction, as much for the elements set in relation as for the relay mode relentlessly evolving.

We reassure ourselves with this overly vague idea: that Relation diversifies forms of humanity according to infinite strings of models infinitely brought into contact and relayed. This point of departure does not even allow us to outline a typology of these contacts or of the interactions thus triggered. Its sole merit would lie in proposing that Relation has its source in these contacts and not in itself; that its aim is not Being, a self-important entity that would locate its beginning in itself.

Relation is a product that in turn produces. What it produces does not partake of Being. That is why, without too much anthropomorphic reductiveness perhaps, we can risk individuating it here as a system, so as to speak about it by name.

(But if we tried to approach the one obvious fact about Being, we would arrive at the expedient point of view that no questioning is possible—because Being cannot bear having any interaction attached to it. Being is self-sufficient, whereas every question is interactive.)

Prime elements do not enter into Relation. Any prime element would call up the shadow of Being. Lacking any reductive criteria, the undefinable realities of human cultures are here looked upon as constituents, ingredients, with no possibility of our claiming them as primordial. We have ended up thinking of cultures from a national, ethnic, generic (civilizational) angle, as "natural" phenomena of the movement of interaction that organizes or scatters the world we have to share.

This way of considering cultures has become widespread through Relation's very involvement. It is through this window that we watch one another reacting together. Before being perceived as the thing urging us into community, culture calls to mind what it is that divides us from all otherness. It is a discriminating factor, with no ostensible discrimination. It specifies without putting aside. This is why cultures are considered the natural elements of Relation, without really calling the latter by name and without, for all that, their constituting its prime elements.

3

Discussing the comparative values of cultures would amount to maintaining that cultural values are stable and acknowledged as such.

Contact among cultures infers, however, a relation of uncertainty, in the perception one has or the experience one senses of them. The mere fact of reflecting them in common, in a planetary perspective, inflects the nature and the "projection" of every specific culture contemplated. Decisive mutations in the quality of relationships result from this, with spectacular consequences that are often thus "experienced" long before the basis for the change itself has been perceived by the collective consciousness.

For example, the placid, traditional belief in the superiority of written languages over oral languages has long since begun to be challenged. Writing no longer is, nor does it appear to be, any guarantee of transcendence. The first result of this was a widespread appetite for works of folklore, sometimes wrongly considered to be bearers of truth or authenticity; but then came a dramatic effort on the part of most oral languages to become fixed—that is, to become akin to writing, at the very instant that the latter was losing its absolute quality. Behind this change is the oral/written relationship; its first, spectacular result, giving no clear indication of the interaction, was the resurgence of folklores.

Henceforth, one of the least disputed measures of "civilization"—technological capability, with its basis in mastery of sciences and control of economic factors—will find itself branded as something negative (the catastrophes of the sorcerer's apprentice). Ecological protests (which the generic anxieties of the science of ecology have led up to) have taken up this interrupted cry even more resoundingly.

Cultures develop in a single planetary space but to different "times." It would be impossible to determine either a real chronological order or an unquestionable hierarchical order for these times.

One of the results of current cultural processes is a widespread anxiety magnifying worries about the future we must contemplate together; this is everywhere translated into a need for futurologies. Never, until this contemporary period, did any individual culture experience such an intense obsession with the future. The passion for astrology, the predictions and prophesies that were Assyrian or Babylonian in origin and that spread most actively, perhaps during the European Middle Ages, were far more the products of a synthesizing or magical thought than anything produced by concerns about really safeguarding the future. The same held true for the Mayans and Aztecs or in ancient China. Nor did the notion of progress, so much touted by Victor Hugo, take shape as motifs of anticipation. These days futurology is an obsession that tends to set itself up as a science. But any possible laws of such a science would be stamped by the same principle of uncertainty that governs the *métissage* of cultures.

Our planetary adventure does not permit us to guess where solutions to the problems born in precipitate contact between cultures will arise. This is why we cannot put a hierarchical order to the different "times" pressing into this global space. It is not certain that technological time will "succeed," where ethnotechnical time, not yet decided upon by cultures threatened today, would fail. It is not certain that the time of History leads to confluences any faster or more certainly than the diffracted times in which the histories of populations are scattered and call out to one another.

Within this problematic, beyond decisions made by power and domination, nobody knows how cultures are going to react in relation to one another nor which of their elements will be the dominant ones, or thought of as such. In this full-sense all cultures are equal within Relation. And altogether they could not be considered as its prime elements.


4


It is at their undefinable limits, through "precipitate contact," that cultures move. Can we keep them safe, isolate them, "create" them by definition? Can we preserve them from the fallout (pressure or domination) that will take place within them? The tendency, reinforced by how situations are reported, to distinguish between a North and a South, industrialized countries and countries existing in absolute poverty, barely disguises the scorn felt by the former for the latter. Nor does it conceal the pitiless, agreed-upon stakes, maintaining and exacerbating distances; nor, alas, the inability of poor countries on their own, or through decisive effort by those who govern them, to progress beyond the twilight zone of deprivation. But this distinction, sanctioning an established fact, does not permit its full-sense to be completely isolated. As if the observation and the established fact, obeying underground laws, and following their set path, gave rise around them to an indifference of a new sort, which, in fact, is neither egoism nor quite idiocy, and even less is it ignorance or lack of courage. Eroded or standardized forms of sensibility are thus spread, but by both sides at once of the far too visible dividing line.

Those are the facts that the planetary consciousness now forming and fully deculturing must adapt to, confronted by this undecipherable magma.

There are pseudo force-lines, like so many traces that explain too much, prophesied in this maelstrom. Planetary consciousness, manipulated from underground by anyone profiting thereby, creates barriers for itself. By confusing, for example, State and culture, the notion grows that there is such a thing as legitimate States (democracies), a rank to which progress will later lead the effective States reported to be presently places of tyranny and brute violence. An odd lie, one that is simultaneously political and cultural. Violence, which determined which human communities sprang up, today governs the difficult search for some balance in their relations. The question should not be to transform effective States gradually into legitimate States but to work toward

164

making there be an effective state everywhere corresponding to the legitimate state.

What is really legitimate is a culture in apposition to others, one that is permeable and determinant. A culture is what remains after States have passed away or what precedes them of necessity. Cultures can be shared when States have been in confrontation. The limits—the frontiers—of a State can be grasped, but a culture's cannot.

Pseudo force-lines hide—at the same time as they authorize—the real ones. Any expression of these real ones provokes in consciousness an unheard response of rejection. If one forces oneself to be specific about developments in planetary consciousness, one comes closer to one of the dimensions of Relation without ever being in a position to define its characteristics—because unvoiced and hard-to-analyze responses of rejection are just as determinant in such matters as anything with widespread and public assent. The rejection apparatus is all the more effective when pseudo force-lines are imposed elsewhere through the proliferation of glamorous fashions that provide an illusion of fruitful innovation. The succession of rapidly passing fashions, embodiment and lure of a passion for the new, is put forth as the only guarantee of progress toward reality. It apparently makes any patient attempts at imagining Relation obsolete. It would seem that experiencing Relation, even if caricaturally, abusively, or superficially, whether manic or totally devoured, would be enough to sustain it. And that attempts at dealing with it in some sustained manner would fall into the category of a pedantic pomposity that is completely foreign to its exacerbated content.

What we call actuality or current events in part is none other than this transience of fashions, taken to the utmost degree of exasperation by an infinite number of agents of commotion, flash agents.

165

What is a flash agent? To conceive the question we must first consider the age-old ways in which cultures have interacted each time they have been in contact. Not just the interaction of their tendencies toward attraction or repulsion but the workings of their inner structures that become modified each time—the network of similarity or osmosis, or rejection or renaturing, that formed, manifested itself, canceled itself out, simply because of what could have been called relay agents. Formerly (and by agreement), these relay agents needed relative obscurity, like a latency period, in relation to their perception of the results of their action—to really work. The relay agent was active because, first of all, he went unnoticed.

Today flash agents are the relay agents who are in tune with the implicit violence of contacts between cultures and the lightning speed of techniques of relation. They send consciousness hurtling into the sudden certainty that it is in possession of the obvious keys of interaction or, usually, into the assurance that it does not need such keys. They dictate fashion and commonplace—these two modern embodiments of interrelation.

If these risky keys (fashion and commonplace) seem to us so very obvious, it is because the flash agents impress us especially through the immediacy (pure pressure) of their communication techniques. Their action is sufficient unto itself here; there is no stated ideology of communication. The ones in control of it in the world do not even have to justify this control. They plainly sanction it just by the fact that communication is continuously in flux: that is, its "freedom" made legitimate by its topicality, that is, its transience.

Relay agents, today transformed into flash agents, tend thus to reject as inoperable two notions that were formerly of major importance: the idea of structure and that of ideology. The transformation of relay into flash strikes at the weak point of these two notions: their overemphasized generalizations in space and time. They too, the idea of structure and the idea of ideology, also required a latency period to shed some light on what they were about. The violent haste of the present offers them a challenge. Fashion sends the analysis inferred by ideology drastically off course, and the commonplace scatters the intent preserved in structure's thought— or, at least, this is what they fiercely claim to do.

# Relinked, (Relayed), Related

## 1

It would be impossible to maintain that each particular culture constitutes a prime element among all those activated in Relation, since the latter defines the elements thus at stake, and at the same time it affects (changes) them. Nor could it be asserted that each particular culture is plainly knowable in its particularity, since its proper limit is not discernible in Relation.

Each particular culture is impelled by the knowledge of its particularity, but this knowledge is boundless. By the same token one cannot break each particular culture down into prime elements, since its limit is not defined and since Relation functions both in this internal relationship (that of each culture to its components) and, at the same time, in an external relationship (that of this culture to others that affect it).

Definition of the internal relationship is never-ending, in other words unrecognizable in turn, because the components of a culture, even when located, cannot be reduced to the indivisibility of prime elements. But such a definition is a working model. It allows us to imagine.

Definition of the external relationship could be infinitely analyzed as well, because, not being plainly composed of prime—indivisible—elements, no particular culture in turn can be considered as a prime element in Relation. The result is that we come back to our original propositions, completing the circle—the round—of our space-time. Paradoxically, every breakthrough toward a definition of this external relationship (between cultures) permits us a better approach to the components of each of the particular cultures considered.

Analysis helps us to imagine better; the imaginary then helps us to grasp the (not prime) elements of our totality.

Case by case and society after society, the humanities, from anthropology to sociology, have studied these structural components and dynamic relationships. But none of these disciplines forms any conception of the overall rhythm, though without their work this would be inaccessible.

If we carry over these two movements (internal and external relationship) to certain presuppositions of thought, the assessment, perhaps, will be that the former is determined by something related to the physical nature of beings, whereas the latter would follow a course that amounts to an approach to Being.

The internal relay would be massive, operating directly, whereas the external relation would be evasive (expanded), too swift in any case for any possibility of grasping its laws of operation at the moment that they apply.

We shall guard against suggesting, parabolically, that beings would be solid and Being volatile nor that a variable mass of beings would assume, in contrast, the infinity of Being. We must, rather, abandon this apposition of Being and beings: renounce the fruitful maxim whereby Being is relation, to consider that Relation alone is relation.

But Relation is not to be confused with the cultures we are discussing nor with the economy of their internal relationships nor with the projection of their external relationships nor even with the intangible results of the intricate involvement of all internal relationships with all possible external

170

relationships. Nor is it to be confused with some marvelous accident that might suddenly occur apart from any relationship, the known unknown, in which chance would be the magnet. Relation is all these things at once.

The genesis of a particular culture could be grasped and its specificity approached without having to be defined. The genesis of Relation cannot be approached, whereas the definition of it can be, if not decided, at least imagined.

If one misjudged the intensity of the particularity of a culture, if one meant to deny the particular value of any culture, for example, in the name of the universality of an All, the implication would be either that Relation has its principle in itself (it would be the universal in-itself and only that) or else that it relays afferents providing one another with mutual reference and consequently leading not to totality but to the totalitarian.

The totalitarian is introduced into relation on the basis of some nonprime element (violence, for example, or race) whose definition is overdetermined but knowledge of which, nonetheless, has limits. This totalitarian relation is, in turn, approachable, but its definition cannot be imagined. Because one cannot imagine a relation—open—among elements the knowledge of which has boundaries. Totality, on the other hand, like Relation, is not approached, but its definition is imaginable.

The difference between Relation and totality lies in the fact that Relation is active within itself, whereas totality, already in its very concept, is in danger of immobility. Relation is open totality; totality would be relation at rest. Totality is virtual. Actually, only rest could, in itself, be legitimately or totally virtual. For movement is precisely that which realizes itself absolutely. Relation is movement.

Not only does Relation not base its principles on itself (rather with and through the elements whose relationship it conducts), but also these principles must be supposed to change as rapidly as the elements thus put into play define (embody) new relationships and change them.

Let us repeat this, chaotically: Relation neither relays nor links afferents that can be assimilated or allied only in their principle, for the simple reason that it always differentiates among them concretely and diverts them from the totalitarian—because its work always changes all the elements composing it and, consequently, the resulting relationship, which then changes them all over again.

2

Relation, as we have emphasized, does not act upon prime elements that are separable or reducible. If this were true, it would itself be reduced to some mechanics capable of being taken apart or reproduced. It does not precede itself in its action and presupposes no a priori. It is the boundless effort of the world: to become realized in its totality, that is, to evade rest. One does not first enter Relation, as one might enter a religion. One does not first conceive of it the way we have expected to conceive of Being.

3

The thing that makes the understanding of every culture limitless is precisely the thing that allows us to imagine, without approaching it, the infinite interaction of cultures. Magma in profusion, tending to empty all thought of ideology, which is considered inapplicable to such an amalgam. Collective drives tend more toward the literal and utilitarian (the reassuring heft of concrete results promoted to the dignity of a value) or toward the providential and ideal (the reassuring determination of a cause or hero making choices for you). Literal and ideal make good company for each other.

Repressed in this manner, ideological thought (the need to analyze, understand, transform) invents new forms for itself and plays tricks with profusion: it projects itself into futurology, which also has no limits. It attempts, for example, to create a synthesis with likely applications from the sciences, which gradually leads into theories of model making. The models claim to base the matter of Relation in relationships; in other words, they claim to catch its movement in the act and then translate this in terms of dynamic or energized structures.

Thus, ideological thought and structural thought come together in their use of models to protest against the amalgam's mixing action. Making models is a (generalizing) attempt to get beyond the transient currency of fashion and the falsely definitive obviousness of the commonplace.


4


Relation relinks (relays), relates. Domination and resistance, osmosis and withdrawal, the consent to dominating language (*langage*) and defense of dominated languages (*langues*).[1] They do not add up to anything clearcut or easily perceptible with any certainty. The relinked (relayed), the related, cannot be combined conclusively. Their mixing in nonappearance (or depth) shows nothing revealing on the surface. This revealer is set astir when the poetics of Relation calls upon the imagination. What best emerges from Relation is what one senses.

By the same token, whenever we try to analyze Relation, the analysis as such being in turn an element of relation, it seems pointless to grant every new proposition in a succession of convincing examples. The example only bears a relationship to one element of a multiple whose parts are in harmony with and repel one another in many areas at once. Choosing one example (introducing it as evidence, using it for demonstration) also unduly privileges one of these areas: misperceiving relationship within Relation.

The accumulation of examples is reassuring to us but is outside of any claim to system. Relation cannot be "proved," because its totality is not approachable. But it can be imagined, conceivable in transport of thought. The accumulation of examples aims at perfecting a never complete description of the processes of relation, not circumscribing them or giving legitimacy to some impossible global truth. In this sense the most harmonious analysis is the one that poetically describes flying or diving. Description is no proof; it simply adds something to Relation insofar as the latter is a synthesis-genesis that never is complete.

5

Cultures coincide in the historic precipitousness (the confluence of histories) that has become their commonplace. There is no point now to the vast expanses of time (let us get back to this) that formerly allowed slow, deep sedimentations to accumulate gradually. They used to authorize, unheeded, thus all the more decisive contacts whose quality of interrelation was not immediately forseeable or measurable, in the same way that haste today distracts us, spreading out before our eyes the networks of causality whose workings we might have been able to discover. The results of unheeded contact became as essential as original elements, just as if only the internal movement of a particular culture had caused them—an infinite and undefinable movement.

Industrialized nations have long beat time for this precipitousness, determining its speed and giving rhythm to trends, through the control they exert over modes of power and means of communication. The situation worldwide "integrates" cultures becoming exhausted by this speed and others that are stuck somewhere off by themselves. The latter are kept in a state of sluggish, passive receptivity in which fantasies of spectacular development and overwhelming consumption remain fantasies.

An important principle of the process of interaction is that its force lines can be reported without the report ever having any effect. Contemporary flash agents (radios, newspapers, televisions, films, and their by-products) have long ceased to be capable of producing such effects, but this is because they spread the radiance of their own dazzle, which is only the reflection of force lines that go unnoticed. For that matter this is possibly the quickest route to identifying the lines of force thus revealed (identification being made not through reflection but through the sort of diffracted provocation that is the mark of these agents).

What is apparently an infinite regression (the accumulation of commonplaces that are publicly shared and celebrated in ephemeral rituals) thus withstands the presumed barbaric nature of fashion but at the same time delineates the evolving depth of Relation. It is no longer easy to spot the possible influence of any group of individuals or works belonging to an "elite," except at the limited stage of some technical or scientific specialization that is tacitly recognized

175

without verification. Proof by elite has ceased to count. The enormous divagation replacing it leaves no time for retreat or re-seizure.

Such an analysis, whose gears start to engage at the place where flash agents are generated (roughly, the industrialized countries), is absolutely valid for those subjected to its imposition (roughly, the countries existing in absolute poverty).

We will never be able to list all the commonplaces echoing throughout Relation: an idea rerun across many, in principle, heterogeneous fields; repetitions (in a rudimentary and caricatural but immediately triumphant form) by flash agents of some reflected-upon information, which moreover had gone under and vanished just because it was a reflection, that is, suspiciously deep; baroque assemblages of force lines that intensify in unexpected places, etc.

The commonplace (defined as the manifestation by some flash agent of a major, latent, or unsuspected line of force) thus immediately acquires a neutral power whose side effects are spectacle and swift passage. Even the very notion of fashion is outrun at this speed. Indeed, what we have is a sequence of moments of inebriation whose sense no fashion could fathom. Commonplaces are rambling, ephemeral particles within communication, this cold nodule; all the ideas are in the air, but it is the public manifestation of these (pushed, whenever possible, to the limit or simplified) that counts. (Thus, the commonplace, *lieu-commun*, with its hyphen in French between the two terms articulating and constituting it, is the spectacular manifestation of this open and mysterious poetic necessity—the common place.)[2] What is public, therefore, is first spectacular. The conclusion is immediately obvious: the cultures apart,* who are receivers of this manifestation of the spectacular but not its generators, have no thought that counts.

A particular culture can pretend to function off on the

*Apart is not the same as what was formerly peripheral: it refers to de facto dependence, no longer a dependence by Law.

176

sidelines (because of being cut off from relay lines or because it has no flash agents or because it chose, defining its own dazzle to scorn such lines), but it nonetheless plays a part— because things couldn't be otherwise—as an active relay of Relation.

The relaying action of cultures does not depend on their will or even their power to relay. The consequences of the succession of relays go beyond the occasion of the first relay, or the original relay, which claimed to have started it all. The inadequacy of this claim is revealed when the sequence stops or becomes realized in another area or another cycle. This is why Relation, which is the world's newness, drives every possible fashion faster and faster. In contrast with the parade of fashions, Relation does not present itself as anything new. Indiscriminately, it is newness.

<br>

6

<br>

Any presence—even though it is ignored—of a particular culture, even a silent one, is an active relay in Relation. Could passive relays exist? Of course not, but in any case there are neutral relays. A factor that is consumed in its own dazzle: the intervention of one State on the territory of another, genocide, the universal triumph of a way of life, generalization of a standardized product, humanitarian aid, an international institution, commercial exchange on a large or small scale, the ritual demonstration of sports gatherings, the great planetary swell of gut-wrenching music. . . . All these are direct agents, in fact, but ones whose relay is not directly perceived to the extent that what is spectacular about the agent overrides the continuum of its effect, and masks it through the very organization of its spectacle. The difficulty one has in discerning the effects of interaction is what allows one to differentiate between neutral and active agents. A cultural presence can be active and ignored, whereas an intervention can be, on the contrary, spectacular and neutral. Here the neutral is not the ineffective but, rather, what is concealed beneath the spectacle. The active is not dominant; it acts in the continuum.

Flash agents transform into a neutral relay (neutralized in the dazzle of its manifest proofs) the very thing that formerly functioned as an active relay, one not immediately perceived but long rendered dynamic by relay agents.

In consequence, we know what these relay agents are today: they are *échos-monde* working with the matter of Relation. And, conversely, we can define the scope of the tactics of flash agents; they literally reflect this matter, their reflections manifesting its violence without shedding any light on it or shifting it or changing it.

Anyone who wishes to intervene in modes of Relation (coloring, balancing, changing them perhaps) will find his action on unsure footing because of this indeterminacy between active and neutral relays. This is why such an intervention "in Relation" can only really happen "in a place," one simultaneously closed in on its components and open to its returning echoes. There is no generalizable strategy of action in Relation that can be developed. Ideology has increased its "disciplined" efforts to go beyond this stubborn limit, precisely by making generalizations: the proletariat's final role, permanent revolution, a nation's civilizing mission, universal defense of freedom, or even the anticommunist crusade (we have to hope that oppressors of every stripe will soon find this pretext lacking), etc. These attempts at repossession or global action run up against the singularities of Relation every time. Relation is only universal through the absolute and specific quantity of its particularities.*

*The actions that are generalized in reality are hidden there and hard to spot: the actions of multinationals and power plots.

It is the nature of flash agents to keep a distance, to widen the gap between surfacing cultures and cultures of intervention (one of the "undisciplined" forms of the generalizing universal). They wear thought out with the apparatus of its delusion. They divert it toward the certainty that its "end" is to perfect the very thing that reinforces their emergence alone as flash agents and maintains their simultaneously logical and distorting power. They need the gap (between producing countries and recipient countries) to hold to their line.*

It would be a utopian assessment to say that cultures that do not manipulate flash agents would be compensated with some sort of reverse reward in a slow and balanced deepening of their values. While it is true that there is no way of guessing "where the real solutions will spring from," simply having confidence in some sort of future justice would also be presumptuous. Ethnotechnology, for example (the appropriateness of needs and means within a given place), will not have enough "natural" apparatus to force itself anywhere: its agents are neutral and powerless; its aim runs out of steam and in the long run wears thin in the dazzling diffraction of the flash agents. There is no escaping the precipitousness of history, even if, through force or inclination, one keeps one's distance when it avalanches.

---

*It would seem that, strictly corresponding to the old division between the discoverers and the discovered, there is now a redivision between producer countries and recipient countries, except for Japan. But let us repeat that this redivision is no longer the result of law; it sanctions a de facto domination, one not based on any privilege of knowledge nor on any claim to be absolute.

179

# V

## POETICS

*Beings, multiple infinite in subsistence*

# GENERALIZATION

*Recognizing, imagining, Relation.*
*Yet another undertaking, thoroughly disguised, of univer-*
*salizing generalization?*
*Escape, the problems at our heels?*
*No imagination helps avert destitution in reality, none can*
*oppose oppressions or sustain those who "withstand" in body*
*or spirit. But imagination changes mentalities, however slowly*
*it may go about this.*

*No matter where one is, no matter how strong the force of*
*errantry, one can hear the mounting desire to "give-on-and-*
*with," to discover order in chaos or at least to guess its unlikely*
*motivation: to develop this theory that would escape*
*generalizations.*

*Poetics? Precisely this double thrust, being a theory that tries to*
*conclude, a presence that concludes (presumes) nothing. Never*
*one without the other. That is how the instant and duration*
*comfort us.*
*Every poetics is a palliative for eternity.*

# That Those Beings Be Not Being

## 1

"Being is relation": but Relation is safe from the idea of Being.

The idea of relation does not limit Relation, nor does it fit outside of it.

The idea of relation does not preexist (Relation).

Someone who thinks Relation thinks by means of it, just as does someone who thinks he is safe from it.

Relation contaminates, sweetens, as a principle, or as flower dust.

Relation enferals, lying in wait for equivalence.

That which would preexist (Relation) is vacuity of Being-as-Being.

Being-as-Being is not opaque but self-important.

Relation struggles and states itself in opacity. It defers self-importance.

Whatever claims to preexist it is insufficient, that is self-importance for itself.

Being-as-Being is sufficiency for itself.

For which reason it is the echo of the idea of Being.

Relation does not assert Being, except to distract.

Also, when put forward in Relation, every assertion is a limit.

For Relation neither deteriorates through nor obliterates any regression. Its patience outdistances depths and sea.

Thus Relation is idea of Being but scatters abroad from Being-as-Being and confronts presence.


2


Beings remain, as long as Being dissipates.

Relation scatters from Being, asserts the subject.

To himself the subject is a thick cloud of knowledge.

That is why Relation also dismantles the thought of non-Being.

That is why it is not: (of) Being, but:—(of) beings.

Non-Being could not be except outside Relation.

Non-Being does not precede Relation, which is not expressed on the basis of any break.

The nonbeing of Relation would be its impossible completion.


3


Beings, which subsist and present themselves, are not merely substance, which would be sufficient unto itself.

Beings risk the being of the world, or being-earth.

The being of the world realizes Being:—in beings.

The being of the world cannot be divided from the being of the universe and whatever imagines itself suspended in this whole. This suspension is not primarily spatial.

The being of the world is total and limited. Its imagination varies; its knowledge flows.

Relation is the knowledge in motion of beings, which risks the being of the world.

Relation strives toward the being of the universe, through consent or violence. This effort is not primarily spatial.

Never conceive of the being of the world or the being of the universe as being of Being or fitting themselves to it.

It depends upon Relation that the knowledge in motion of the being of the universe be granted through osmosis, not through violence.

Relation comprehends violence, marks its distance.

It is passage, not primarily spatial, that passes itself off as passage and confronts the imaginary.

# For Opacity

Several years back, if I made the statement, "We demand the right to opacity," or argued in favor of this, whoever I was speaking to would exclaim indignantly: "Now it's back to barbarism! How can you communicate with what you don't understand?" But in 1989, and before very diverse audiences, when the same demand was formulated, it aroused new interest. Who knows? Maybe, in the meanwhile, the topicality of the question of differences (the right to difference) had been exhausted.

The theory of difference is invaluable. It has allowed us to struggle against the reductive thought produced, in genetics for example, by the presumption of racial excellence or superiority. Albert Jacquard (*Éloge de la différence*, Éditions du Seuil, 1978) dismantled the mechanisms of this barbaric notion and demonstrated how ridiculous it was to claim a "scientific" basis for them. (I call the reversal and exasperation of self barbaric and just as inconceivable as the cruel results of these mechanisms.) This theory has also made it possible to take in, perhaps, not their existence but at least the rightful entitlement to recognition of the minorities swarming throughout the world and the defense of their status. (I call "rightful" the escape far from any legitimacy anchored silently or resolutely in possession and conquest.)

But difference itself can still contrive to reduce things to the Transparent.

If we examine the process of "understanding" people and

189

ideas from the perspective of Western thought, we discover that its basis is this requirement for transparency. In order to understand and thus accept you, I have to measure your solidity with the ideal scale providing me with grounds to make comparisons and, perhaps, judgments. I have to reduce.[1]

Accepting differences does, of course, upset the hierarchy of this scale. I understand your difference, or in other words, without creating a hierarchy, I relate it to my norm. I admit you to existence, within my system. I create you afresh. —But perhaps we need to bring an end to the very notion of a scale. Displace all reduction.

Agree not merely to the right to difference but, carrying this further, agree also to the right to opacity that is not enclosure within an impenetrable autarchy but subsistence within an irreducible singularity. Opacities can coexist and converge, weaving fabrics. To understand these truly one must focus on the texture of the weave and not on the nature of its components. For the time being, perhaps, give up this old obsession with discovering what lies at the bottom of natures. There would be something great and noble about initiating such a movement, referring not to Humanity but to the exultant divergence of humanities. Thought of self and thought of other here become obsolete in their duality. Every Other is a citizen and no longer a barbarian. What is here is open, as much as this there. I would be incapable of project-ing from one to the other. This-here is the weave, and it weaves no boundaries. The right to opacity would not estab-lish autism; it would be the real foundation of Relation, in freedoms.

And now what they tell me is, "You calmly pack your poetics into these craters of opacity and claim to rise so serenely beyond the prodigiously elucidating work that the West has accomplished, but there you go talking nonstop about this West." —"And what would you rather I talk about at the beginning, if not this transparency whose aim was to reduce us? Because, if I don't begin there, you will see me consumed with the sullen jabber of childish refusal, convulsive and powerless. This is where I start. As for my identity, I'll take care of that myself." There has to be dialogue with the West, which, moreover is contradictory in itself (usually this is the argument raised when I talk about cultures of the One); the complementary discourse of whoever wants to give-on-and-with must be added to the West. And can you not see that we are implicated in its evolution?

Merely consider the hypothesis of a Christian Europe, convinced of its legitimacy, rallied together in its reconstituted universality, having once again, therefore, transformed its forces into a "universal" value—triangulated with the technological strength of the United States and the financial sovereignty of Japan—and you will have some notion of the silence and indifference that for the next fifty years (if it is possible thus to estimate) surround the problems, the dependencies and the chaotic sufferings of the countries of the south with nothingness.

And also consider that the West itself has produced the variables to contradict its impressive trajectory every time. This is the way in which the West is not monolithic, and this is why it is surely necessary that it move toward entanglement. The real question is whether it will do so in a participatory manner or if its entanglement will be based on old impositions. And even if we should have no illusions about the realities, their facts already begin to change simply by asking this question.

The opaque is not the obscure, though it is possible for it to be so and be accepted as such. It is that which cannot be reduced, which is the most perennial guarantee of participation and confluence. We are far from the opacities of Myth or Tragedy, whose obscurity was accompanied by exclusion and whose transparency aimed at "grasping." In this version of understanding the verb *to grasp* contains the movement of

191

hands that grab their surroundings and bring them back to themselves. A gesture of enclosure if not appropriation. Let our understanding prefer the gesture of giving-on-and-with that opens finally on totality.

At this point I need to explain what I mean by this totality I have made so much noise about. It is the idea itself of totality, as expressed so superbly in Western thought, that is threatened with immobility. We have suggested that Relation is an open totality evolving upon itself. That means that, thought of in this manner, it is the principle of unity that we subtract from this idea. In Relation the whole is not the finality of its parts: for multiplicity in totality is totally diversity. Let us say this again, opaquely: the idea of totality alone is an obstacle to totality.

We have already articulated the poetic force. We see it as radiant—replacing the absorbing concept of unity; it is the opacity of the diverse animating the imagined transparency of Relation. The imaginary does not bear with it the coercive requirements of idea. It prefigures reality, without determining it a priori.

The thought of opacity distracts me from absolute truths whose guardian I might believe myself to be. Far from cornering me within futility and inactivity, by making me sensitive to the limits of every method, it relativizes every possibility of every action within me. Whether this consists of spreading overarching general ideas or hanging on to the concrete, the law of facts, the precision of details, or sacrificing some apparently less important thing in the name of efficacy, the thought of opacity saves me from unequivocal courses and irreversible choices.

As far as my identity is concerned, I will take care of it myself. That is, I shall not allow it to become cornered in any essence; I shall also pay attention to not mixing it into any amalgam. Rather, it does not disturb me to accept that there are places where my identity is obscure to me, and the fact that it amazes me does not mean I relinquish it. Human

192

behaviors are fractal in nature. If we become conscious of this and give up trying to reduce such behaviors to the obviousness of a transparency, this will, perhaps, contribute to lightening their load, as every individual begins not grasping his own motivations, taking himself apart in this manner. The rule of action (what is called ethics or else the ideal or just logical relation) would gain ground—as an obvious fact—by not being mixed into the preconceived transparency of universal models. The rule of every action, individual or community, would gain ground by perfecting itself through the experience of Relation. It is the network that expresses the ethics. Every moral doctrine is a utopia. But this morality would only become a utopia if Relation itself had sunk into an absolute excessiveness of Chaos. The wager is that Chaos is order and disorder, excessiveness with no absolute, fate and evolution.

I thus am able to conceive of the opacity of the other for me, without reproach for my opacity for him. To feel in solidarity with him or to build with him or to like what he does, it is not necessary for me to grasp him. It is not necessary to try to become the other (to become other) nor to "make" him in my image. These projects of transmutation—without metempsychosis—have resulted from the worst pretensions and the greatest of magnanimities on the part of West. They describe the fate of Victor Segalen.

The death of Segalen is not just a physiological outcome. We recall his confiding, in the last days of his life, about the slovenliness of his body, whose illness he was unable to diagnose and whose decline he was unable to control. No doubt it will be known, with a list of his symptoms and the help of medical progress, what he died of. And no doubt the people around him could say he died of some sort of generalized consumption. But I myself believe that he died of the opacity of the Other, of coming face to face with the impossibility of accomplishing the transmutation that he dreamed of.

Like every European of his day, he was marked with a substantial, even if unconscious, dose of ethnocentrism. But he was also possessed, more than any of his contemporaries, by this absolute and incomplete generosity that drove him to realize himself elsewhere. He suffered from this accursed contradiction. Unable to know that a transfer into transparency ran counter to his project and that, on the contrary, respect for mutual forms of opacity would have accomplished it, he was heroically consumed in the impossibility of being Other. Death is the outcome of the opacities, and this is why the idea of death never leaves us.

On the other hand, if an opacity is the basis for a Legitimacy, this would be the sign of its having entered into a political dimension. A formidable prospect, less dangerous perhaps than the erring ways to which so many certainties and so many clear, so-called lucid truths have led. The excesses of these political assurances would fortunately be contained by the sense not that everything is futile but that there are limits to absolute truth. How can one point out these limits without lapsing into skepticism or paralysis? How can one reconcile the hard line inherent in any politics and the questioning essential to any relation? Only by understanding that it is impossible to reduce anyone, no matter who, to a truth he would not have generated on his own. That is, within the opacity of his time and place. Plato's city is for Plato, Hegel's vision is for Hegel, the griot's town is for the griot. Nothing prohibits our seeing them in confluence, without confusing them in some magma or reducing them to each other. This same opacity is also the force that drives every community: the thing that would bring us together forever and make us permanently distinctive. Widespread consent to specific opacities is the most straightforward equivalent of nonbarbarism.

We clamor for the right to opacity for everyone.

# Open Circle, Lived Relation

There is a point at which Relation is no longer expressed through a procession of trajectories, itineraries succeeding or thwarting one another, but explodes by itself and within itself, like a network, inscribed in the self-sufficient totality of the world.

We leave behind the imaginary that projects, with its daring inventions, its escapades, the unknown things it has risked: flaming arrows and unmerciful shots. The thrust of the world and its desire no longer embolden you onward in a fever of discovery: they multiply you all around.

Having in the end, and despite all the impossibilities, drawn near Relation and acknowledged our presentiments of how it works, now we must disindividuate it as a system, stretch it to the mass that bursts forth just from its energy, finding ourselves there along with others.

To disindividuate Relation is to relate the theory to the lived experience of every form of humanity in its singularity. This means returning to the opacities, which produce every exception, are propelled by every divergence, and live through becoming involved not with projects but with the reflected density of existences.

What we call the world today is not only the convergence of the histories of peoples that has swept away the claims of philosophies of History but also the encounters (in consciousness) among these histories and materialities of the planet. Catastrophic fires reactivate the work of genocides; famines and droughts take root in suicidal political regimes; warring parties defoliate on a staggering scale; floods and hurricanes call forth international solidarity, yet no one can prevent them or really combat their effects; humanitarian movements that have sprung up in wealthy nations strive to bandage the open sores in poor countries, inflicted more often than not by the merciless economies of these same rich countries; jungles and tribes are simultaneously torn up by the roots; and so it goes on endlessly. The shock wave set off in the European consciousness by the earthquake in Lisbon in the eighteenth century has spread far and wide. No specific history (joy or tragedy, extortion or liberation) is shut up solely in its own territory nor solely in the logic of its collective thought. The woes of the landscape have invaded speech, rekindling the woes of humanities, in order to conceive of it. Can we bear ad infinitum this rambling on of knowledge? Can we get our minds off it? Here the imaginary of totality saves us from escheat—from reverted errantry.

If, however, we mean to escape either vague rambling or the neutralizing tactics of suspension we ordinarily use to avoid it, we must not just imagine totality as we earlier suggested nor simply approach Relation through a displacement of thought; we must also involve this imaginary in the place we live, even if errantry is part of it. Neither action nor place are generalizable.

What I said about *antillanité,* in this place where we, men and women of the Caribbean, rise up, represents quite simply the will to rally together and diffract the Ante-Islands confirming us in ourselves and joining us to an elsewhere. For us *antillanité,* a method and not a state of being, can never be accomplished, nor can we go beyond it.

But though we are thus entering modernity, by confirming the work of our cultures, we cannot be unaware that one of modernity's most persistent motifs is wholly embodied in the unconscious drive that wills deculturation. Because humanities sense that their cultures constitute the (not prime) elements of the generality of *chaos-monde,* they instinctively indulge in anticultural backlash. As if they wanted to preserve this generality from any normative effects that the culture's thought might have introduced. (Moreover, it doesn't matter how we stigmatize one episode or another, for example, of the Chinese Revolution, when the entire apparatus of flash agents aims for the same anticultural elementarity.) As if they meant to assert that cultures do not delineate preestablished harmonies, that the histories of peoples do not all work toward a single genealogy.[1] Modern violence is anticultural, which means it tries hard to guarantee the open energy of the shock between cultures. Is this a return of barbarism, or is it some prophetic precautionary measure against the barbarism of reductiveness and uniformity?

One of the constants of this modern violence is that its duty is to be staged at all costs. Whether this modern violence is real or simulated, it demands to shine and cannot do without the services of flash agents. The underground violences, in the ghettos or in the bush, the violences of obscure wars for survival, come unraveled when solutions appear. The blacks in the United States, in the places where they are the poorest, because they are the poorest, because the means of existence are beyond them, and because they have no other solutions, exert a total violence in the city underground. The violence of destitute poverty is not, however, a mission. But modern violence, born of the shock among cultures, is of another sort. It feeds on its own dazzle and is exacerbated by its own feedback.

Two of the television shows that struck me most in the United States, in a surprising parallel, present a mixture of belief, intensified by its own spectacle and by a willingness to believe, which is kept up beyond any approximations of spectacle. Wrestling matches are not really meant to determine which competitor is the strongest. In the audience, however, they stir up waves of irrepressible violence, stripped of any skepticism. This is not a matter of displaying only bestial violence but, going much further, a pure (if one can call it that) violence, white as metal heated to the most intense incandescence. The audience believes in this violence, in its spectacle; it comes for that. It comes in families, with children. It does not care that staging conceals the cheating. The desire for manifest violence is stronger than any suspicion of hidden nonviolence. The alarming costumes of the wrestlers, the incredibly heightened language that they engage in during the televised interviews heralding their fights and serving to advertise them, the surge of pretend or real sadism onstage, all make it perfectly obvious that the rule here is to produce the severest shock possible.

There is another spectacle that is just as astounding because of its suppressed violence: TV preaching. These preachers give a physical performance, making the most of the body's every posture. They imitate the extremely effective gestures of black actors, they weep, they sing, they play the piano, they turn the voltage as high as it will go and keep the physical and spiritual tension up relentlessly before resolving it in a blessed beatitude. Those present (and perhaps also the television viewers?) all weep in unison, faint, and go into trances. That the preaching is staged does not bother anyone nor do the scandals concerning the behavior and corrupt practices that have sullied a number of these dazzling ministers, these flash preachers. The desire for catharsis is stronger than any suspicion of insincerity.

Asceticism through violence, in order to rediscover an original purity. You have to show that you abandon yourself to it and that this works. This is not yet the violence of barbarism but a desperate quest. Barbarism (tyrannical self-love) comes later. That is why such powerful personal generosities exist in this country: they are an endeavor to fend off the convulsions of the maelstrom. Although the social service laws are ridiculously inadequate here compared with the various European legislations in force, nowhere else in the world does a call for gifts and private contributions encounter such a response, frequently verging on naïveté. The violence of deculturation is thus somehow domesticated: caught up in dailiness.

Let us not stop with this commonplace: that a poetics cannot guarantee us a concrete means of action. But a poetics, perhaps, does allow us to understand better our action in the world. We consider, for instance, how our requirement for cultural responsibility, inseparable from political independence, is to be related to the prophylactic violence of forms of deculturation. Put into Relation. That is what one might call "defolkloration." The reductions of folklore (the belief that only atavistic energies will provide an existence) lie in ambush for all cultures, whether or not they are technological. The awareness of modernity leads us away from this reductiveness, offering us the image of relations, similarities of situation or diverging directions, between what is us and what is other.

But we must also examine the need to be careful, because every generalization gives birth to its illusions.[2] For example: though folklore debilitates, it just as powerfully creates rhizomes. One could say that modernity, when it puts us thus in a position to be relative without being lost, coadjusts without confusing.

What means do we have at our disposal to balance these requirements, which are not necessarily harmonic?

First, the imaginary. It works in a spiral: from one circularity to the next, it encounters new spaces and does not transform them into either depths or conquests. Nor is it confined to the binarities that have seemed to preoccupy me throughout this book: extension/filiation, transparency/opacity[3] . . . The imaginary becomes complete on the margins of every new linear projection. It creates a network and constitutes volume. Binarities only serve as conveniences for approaching its weave.

The imaginary comments with a dirge, or it just giggles. Usually, approaching the *chaos-monde* in all its turbulence, it is wary of this reserve dimension referred to as humor. Humor always presupposes some hidden reference, providing the humorist his superiority. Humor derives from a classicism left unspoken or, quite the opposite, put in question as in the black humor of the surrealists. But its corrosive power is perhaps dissipated in the turbulence of the *chaos-monde,* in which classicisms do not occur. The Creole storyteller does not want to be a humorist; he is surprising in his talent (which should not be said to be innate) for relentlessly bringing together the most heterogeneous elements of reality. Pierre Reverdy describes the same thing operating in poetry. There is no hidden reference in it but, rather, an uninterrupted process of revelation: of putting into relation. There ought to be some other word to define this bringing together when it astounds us and deflects us from convention.

The preferred scene of the poetics of Relation is plainsong or a yell (in duration or in the instant) because this poetics is disgusted by the offhandedness assumed by any presumption of superiority. In truth, however, this preference does not hold. Baroque speech does not acknowledge any preestablished norm. It recognizes only the rigors of form, precisely because it is confronting excessiveness.

Next, the approach to reality. Conceiving of the order and disorder of the *chaos-monde* does not put you in a privileged position to oppose those who perpetuate their powers of perversion. And yet, if we tried to make a list here concerning loci of hardship and oppression, one of those lists sketched throughout this book about other subjects, this one would surely be the longest. In totality powers reinforce their powers, and it is the weakness of aesthetic thought, of the various specific poetics, that they "make believe" when confronted by this other sort of maelstrom. Though the imaginary of totality may be of no use to anyone in organizing resistance, at least it is possible to think it would allow everyone some protection against the numerous bad habits that are the result of ideology's time-honored thoughts.

How many revolutions, full of how many instances of

going beyond, have not foundered in blind limitations, absurd principles, thus rejoining the things they struggled against? The poetic perception of the *chaos-monde* leads us to sense a few of the lessons of these many disastrous attempts. As for me, and only for myself, that is, with no pretense of giving a lesson, I would sum up these lessons as follows:

The control of an action is in its act.
The full-sense of an action is in its place.
The future of an action is in Relation.

These three statements are not intended to constitute a law. They mean that, once totality has been conceived of, one could not claim to evoke it a priori in order to intercede in problems here and now but that no solution that is acted upon could, however, ignore or underestimate this totality's activity—which is Relation.

Against those who deal out generalizing lessons. Against ideology content with its own company. Against petty local masters. Against an intolerant, nationalist seclusion. Against those who erect borders. Those obsessed with military power. Those who are the repositories of the collective consciousness. The mouthpieces.

There is no naïveté involved in thus "relativizing" the most particular actions thus within the concrete matter of Relation. Habit cannot be snared at one fell swoop. We are just barely beginning to have some idea of this underground logic that is not imposed as predicates but that subjects us collectively to our contradictions.

Contradictions. The racist Boers of South Africa are in seclusion there. They stubbornly invoke the sacredness of root (though filiation is not exportable), and they are unable to consent to the approaches of Relation. They have taken refuge in the rigidity of Apartheid. Oppressed blacks in this country are the bearers of going beyond. They could have merely withdrawn into the sacred that is Territory (they have an ancestral "right" to it, which is, of course, why a point was made of assigning them reservations on this soil), but the terrible intensity of their struggle leads them, however imperceptibly or chaotically, to encounters with people of mixed blood, with Indians, with whites: it teaches them and inspires them with the sense of Relation. Nelson Mandela is an *écho-monde*. Wherever oppressors, in one form or another, impose themselves, those who are oppressed represent, through their very resistance, the guarantee of such a future, even if it is fragile and threatened.* Meaning well has nothing to do with it but, rather, the demand for totality, that every form of oppression tries to reduce and that every resistance contributes to increasing.

Then words, no one's fiefdom, meet up with the materiality of the world. Relation is spoken.

I was struck by the cover of a magazine (*Paris Match*, May 11, 1989), whose tactics are certainly those of a flash agent), on which I read the caption:

*CHERNOBYL:*
*12 villages to be evacuated,*
*the wolves are returning*
*the pines are blue*

What was the infinite detour taken by this nuclear catastrophe, whose worldwide repercussions were felt among the destitute as well as among the well-to-do, in savanna villages, probably, just as much as in skyscrapers, and which consequently fed the most passively experienced of commonplaces in the planetary consciousness, that led it also to be condensed into what seemed to be an involuntary poem, through which it happened that the world could speak to us?

*Oppressive powers know this very well and attempt to incite "heroes," whether real or mythic, to symbolize their causes. Thus there appear pseudo-*échos-monde,* which Western opinion has apparently become expert at creating.

The landscape forced its way through the dazzling barrier, fixing upon the superficial brilliance this terse scrap of utterance.

The circle opens up once more, at the same time that it builds in volume. Thus, at every moment Relation becomes complete but also is destroyed in its generality by exactly what we put into action in a particular time and place. Relation that is destroyed, at every instant and in every circumstance, by this particularity spelling our opacities, through this singularity, becomes once again the experience of relation. Its death as generality is what creates the life it has to share. For, if every group of humankind were to fully live Relation, they would divert the concept into the naturality that would have made it concrete. Relation exists in being realized, that is, in being completed in a common place.

This movement allows giving-on-and-with the dialectic among aesthetics. If the imaginary carries us from thinking about this world to thinking about the universe, we can conceive that aesthetics, by means of which we make our imaginary concrete, with the opposite intention, always brings us back from the infinities of the universe to the definable poetics of our world. This is the world from which all norms are eliminated, and also it is this world that serves as our inspiration to approach the reality of our time and our place. Thus, we go the open circle of our relayed aesthetics, our unflagging politics. We leave the matrix abyss and the immeasurable abyss for this other one in which we wander without becoming lost.

# The Burning Beach

The sand sparkled. Some subterranean (submarine) force repressed what northern volcanoes supplied. The beach is now without cover, without surprises, like a prisoner. Strolling tourists spread their towels on it. Not very many because this is an out-of-the-way spot. Not a single big wave to distract you from the pleasure of lethargy. Order and comfort have timidly returned.

Beneath the conventional image, the kind one sees developed—or summarized—in publicity films in the United States or Japan, the luxuriously fatal image for selling a country ("The Antilles cheap"),* beneath this insipid facade, we rediscover the ardor of a land. I see the mockery of the image, and I do not see it. I catch the quivering of this beach by surprise, this beach where visitors exclaim how beautiful! how typical! and I see that it is burning.

For its background, it has the *mornes*, whose silence can be frightening, the same hills that stand ragged above the *Cohée*, the bay of Lamentin and the devastated mangrove there. They are trying to fill in this mangrove swamp, zoning it for industry or for major centers of consumption. Yet still the swamp resists. My friends took me there, drifting along, looking for hot spots, those redwater muds that gurgle and burn

*The Europeans, in anticipation of the *Acte unique* of 1993, are buying land here without leaving home: they put in their orders and delegate power of attorney.

205

here and there in the mangrove.* The words of the volcano rolling in these mouths come back to me, more meaningful now than when I roamed the place as a child. The same words that used to adorn the sand in dark, penitential vestments, then, bit by bit pulling back, uncovered its luminosity.

This tie between beach and island, which allows us to take off like *marrons,* far from the permanent tourist spots, is thus tied into the dis-appearance—a dis-appearing—in which the depths of the volcano circulate.

I have always imagined that these depths navigate a path beneath the sea in the west and the ocean in the east and that, though we are separated, each in our own Plantation, the now green balls and chains have rolled beneath from one island to the next, weaving shared rivers that we shall open up when it is our time and where we shall take our boats. From where I stand I see Saint Lucia on the horizon. Thus, step by step, calling up the expanse, I am able to realize this seabow.

I am doing the same thing in the way I say *we*—organizing this work around it. Is this some community *we* rhizomed into fragile connection to a place? Or a total *we* involved in the activity of the planet? Or an ideal *we* drawn in the swirls of a poetics?

Who is this intervening *they*? *They* that is Other? or *they* the neighbors? or *they* whom I imagine when I try to speak?

These *we*s and *they*s are an evolving. They find their full-sense, here, in my excessive use of the words *totality* and *Relation.* This excess is repetition that signifies.

They find full-sense in the extension of discourse, in which peremptory abstract notions gain force only through force of

*Bakeries, ironically, are also called "hot spots," *points chauds,* when their bread is delivered by air from France, already shaped into *baguettes,* ready-made *croissants* and *pains au chocolat,* a greenish-gray frozen dough. All the bakery has to do is put them in the microwave . . . to our great delight.

accumulation, since they cannot burn in the body's charcoal fire. The word mass burns, from its amassing.

They find full-sense in the echo of the land, where *morne* meets beach, where the motifs are intertwined in a single vegetation, like words off the page.

Red-earth-red, blacker underneath than the black chalk of our dreams. The clouds of the *Pitons* entangled in enormous ferns, the passionately gray sand where so many volcanoes joined in, the flat stretch of banana trees' dirty lumps of curl, the yam ravines where you can stand up, traces marked along the crests like stubborn sulphur, the light-giving shade of verandas where old and jagged bamboo stirs.

So what comes over us then is neither flash nor revelation but piling up and a vague endlessly repeated impatience.


Suddenly, there is something about the *morne*. A moving on the surface of chaos that changes chaos by its movement. This is not a neutral point; it is not the starting point of a blueprint; it too sends rhizomes into the earth.

(So now, finally, they hint that I have already said all or most of what is said here in *Soleil de la conscience*, that little book published more than thirty years ago. And I agree. We travel on the surface, in the expanse, weaving our imaginary structures and not filling up the voids of a science, but rather, as we go along, removing boxes that are too full so that in the end we can imagine infinite volumes. Volumes like the space sieves invented by the technicians of Chaos that seem filled simply with their own echo.)

(And now here comes the clan of little goats too, leaping morning and evening, to stop off inside the garden wall, invading its grounds and foraging among the sweet bread-fruit and the rotting *prunes de cythère*. Their keeper is right behind them, chasing them toward the dirt road that runs along the beach. The goats' stampeding toward this ritual meal, the shouts of the young goatherd, the circular, disjointed movement, from their hungry storming of the garden to their panicked departure, never changes. And I could never imagine closing the garden gate or banning the animals' detour.)

This shadow on the *morne* all by itself is a school of little goats, rioting in its own noise.

The man who walks (because that's who it is) has soon come down from the hills; once again he is making sense of the beach. His energy is boundless, his withdrawal absolute.

Distant reader, as you recreate these imperceptible details on the horizon, you who can imagine—who can indulge the time and wealth for imagining—so many open and closed places in the world, look at him. Imagine him, falling irreversibly into prostration or suddenly waking up and starting to scream or else gradually succumbing to his family's attentions or all at once going back to his daily route, without further explanation. He signs to you with this bare outline of a movement that precedes all languages. There is so much of the world to be uncovered that you are able to leave this one person alone in his outlook. But he will not leave you. The shadow he throws from a distance is cast close by you.

As for those of us who follow him, if we can put it that way (but we do know the rhythm of his passages; we are able to anticipate them), we are beginning to accept the fact that he is more resistant than we and more lasting than our endless palaver. No one could be content with this enclosed errantry, this circular nomadism—but one with no goal or end or recommencing. The absent man who walks exhausts no territory; he sets roots only in the sacred of the air and evanescence, in a pure refusal that changes nothing in the world. We are not following him in reality, because we always want to change something. But we know in the end that his traveling, which is not nomadism, is also not rambling. It traces repeated figures here on the earth, whose pattern we would catch if we had the means to discover it. This man who walks is an *écho-monde* who is consumed within himself, who represents chaos without realizing it.

The place re-creates its own Plantation, and from it this voice-less voice cries out. Plantations of the world, lonely places of isolation, unnatural enclosures, that you, nonetheless are touching. Mangos, bayous, lagoons, muskegs, ice floes. Ghettos, suburbs, Volga beaches, barrios, crossroads, hamlets, sand trails, river bights. Villages being abandoned, ploughed fields given over to roads, houses shut up against their surroundings, seers bellowing inside their heads.

I leave you now, you who at no point leave the celebration you provide us. Going to acknowledge myself in the unclear and so particular effervescence, of another sort, one with no accumulation of forgetting, and unending because always changing.

The horizon seaweed is interwoven in variations of gray tinged blue with black, where space increases. Their fern makes a rain that does not peel away from the heat of the sky. With the dove gray of thought you touch a tousle of vegetation, a cry of *morne* and red earth. Glowing fires scarcely sparked by dizziness. Rainshower motionless. Dwindling echoes. A tree trunk slivers against the rim of the sun, stubbornness, stiff but melting. Call the keepers of silence with their feet in the river. Call the river that used to spill over the rocks. —As for myself, I have listened to the pulse of these hot spots. I have bathed there beside friends, attentive to the volcano's drums. We have stood bent against the wind without falling. One lone bay; whatever name it had evaporated. Also endeavouring to point out this blue tinge to everything . . . —Its sun strolls by, in the savanna's silver shuddering and the ocre smell of the hounded earth.

# Notes

## ERRANTRY, EXILE

1. While *errance* is usually translated as "wandering," "errantry" seems better suited to Glissant's use of the word, and there is precedence in translations of Césaire. *Errance* for Glissant, while not aimed like an arrow's trajectory, nor circular and repetitive like the nomad's, is not idle roaming, but includes a sense of sacred motivation. *Trans.*
2. The poet Monchoachi organized a series of lectures on the theme of errantry, in Marin, a city in the southern part of Martinique. I was one of the first, I believe, called upon to discuss it in this setting. The Caribbean is a land of rootedness and of errantry. The numerous antillean exiles are evidence of this.
3. Kant, in the *Critique of Pure Reason,* presents what he says about Relation in this manner:

> *Unconditioned unity*
> of RELATION
> that is
> itself, not as inherent
> but as
> SUBSISTENT.
>
> (*Pléiade,* vol. 1; 1468)

Whether this Relation works toward the systematic unity of ends (moral principle) or toward the unity of understandings (architechtonic principle), one can assert here two qualities: first, that it is the binding agent that guarantees the permanence of thought in the individual; and, second, that it has no share in the substance. This difference that Kant seems to establish between substance and subsistence is invaluable. Be that as it may, the idea of Relation for him does not intervene as an opening onto plurality, insofar as it would be a totality. For Kant plurality takes place in time, not in space. In space there is existence, which seems not to be differentiated within itself.

4. The word I have translated here as "rerouting" is *détournement,* one of a number of related words that are important in Glissant's work. (Others are *détourner, détour, retour.*) Usually, I believe that Glissant sees these words in a very active sense, implying a real change of direction. This can be the act of taking another path, or forcing evolution to flow in a different course. It can also be a turning away, or turning aside in a redirection of, or refusal to direct, attention. There are times, for instance, in the slave/master relation when "diversion" in the sense of "providing amusement" was a tactical move on the part of the slave, diverting the master from the slave's actual desires or agenda, but in general I have tried to stress the most active sense. *Trans.*

5. Here Glissant uses the verb *comprendre* in the mechanical sense of including within a system, and *comprehends* is the best translation. In other cases, however, he stresses an almost rapacious quality of the word, its division into two parts based on its Latin roots (i.e. *comprendre:* to take with, which I have translated as "grasps"). He contrasts this with a neologistic phrase: *donner-avec,* which would constitute understanding in Relation. Because, in doing so, he means *donner* both in the sense of generosity and in the sense of "looking out toward" (as in *la fenêtre donne sur la mer*), and because our combining the words *give* and *with* constitutes less a notion of sharing than one of yielding (i.e., "he gave with the blow"), which—though not dominant—is not totally absent from Glissant's usage, *donner-avec* will be translated as "gives-on-and-with." *Trans.*

6. The poetic striving toward totality in no way impugns the minutiae of those who struggle in a given place. The subject matter is not in conflict, and Saint-John Perse does not eclipse Faulkner. Rather, it is possible that the harped-on universal, with which Saint-John Perse so splendidly threw his lot, scatters before Relation, without really coming in contact with it. Generalizing words do not always accompany the cry of the peoples or countries naming themselves.

The spirit of universalization, moreover, is willingly connected with a tendency to deny specific times and histories that are peripheral (Borges or Saint-John Perse), and the aspiration toward this universal tends to disclaim particular spaces and evolutions (V. S. Naipaul).

Numerous writers in our countries strive in similar ways. Rather than dealing with their own fertile imperfections in their works, they revel in the completed and reassuring perfections of the Other. They call them universal. There they find a bitter and legitimate pleasure that gives them the authority to hold themselves above the surroundings in which they might share. The distance they keep from commonality thus leads them to judge quite dispassionately whatever babbles there beside them. But their serene dispassion is strained.

POETICS

1. Glissant's phrase word "full-sense" will appear throughout the text as the translation of *plein-sens*. It indicates a combination of signification, direction, and concrete sensory perception. *Trans.*
2. In *La conquête de l'Amérique* (Editions du Seuil, 1982) (*The Conquest of America: The Question of the Other* [New York: Harper and Row, 1984], trans. Richard Howard) Tzvetan Todorov studied one of the most important manifestations of this relationship between the Same and the Other: that which opposed the American Indians to the Conquistadors. He suggests that when they entered into this relation the Indians reacted with a logic of totality, putting them in a situation of technical inferiority when they confronted the Conquistadors, who acted solely on the basis of a logic of self-interest ("There exist two great forms of communication, one between man and man, the other between man and the world, the Indians cultivated the latter above all, the Spanish the former" [75]). Todorov infers from this that, whereas from the point of view of conquest the Indians, in fact, suffered a defeat that was the prelude to reshaping the Continent and the start of a new history, on the other hand, from the point of view of what I call here a worldwide Relation, their system of reference was the most durable (the most profitable?) one there is. He thus took into account the state of the world, the stage at which we are today, and, in proposing this perception of it, he does not place greater importance on a (Western) "sense" in relation to a (global) content; despite the claim that perhaps he never stopped being

213

dependent upon the "sense" Europe had assigned to the Other (Deborah Root, "The Imperial Signifier: Todorov and the Conquest of Mexico," *Cultural Critique* [Spring 1988]).

3. Following Françoise Lionnet's fine analysis of *métissage* (*Autobiographical Voices: Race, Gender, Self-Portraiture* [Ithaca: Cornell University Press, 1989], 1–29), I have chosen to retain the French term here. The word has a wide range of culturally specific meanings, all value laden. Most English translations, such as *cross-breeding* and *mongrelization*, bear a negative value. (The product, *métis*, is a "half-breed, etc.") *Crossing, braiding*, and *intermixing* are perhaps the most neutral but ignore the problematics of racial difference. *Creolization* works but limits *métissage* to a cultural context. For Glissant *métissage* moves from a narrow range of racial intermixing to become a relational practice affirming the multiplicity and diversity of its components. *Trans.*

4. Meanwhile, a book by Jean Bernabé, Patrick Chamoiseau, and Raphaël Confiant has been published with the title *Eloge de la Créolité* (Paris: Gallimard, 1988). This manifesto attempts to define or proclaim the line of continuity in Martinican literature. This is the work to which I refer when I compare the terms *creolization* and *creoleness*.

5. Summarizing thus:

Oral and written.

The emergence of the languages of orality accompanies a resurgence of spoken poetry, which has become a much more widespread practice, not without numerous shortcomings, of course. Another economy of poetic speech is taking shape, in which recurrence (repetition or redundancy), assonance, variations in tonality, etc., are becoming the approved methods. Maybe writing practices will find themselves rejuvenated by this.

Multilingualism.

The thought of the Center was monolingual. The poetics of Relation requires all the languages of the world. Not to know or to ponder them, but to know (feel) that it is essential for them to exist. That this existence determines the accents of any writing.

Voice-languages (*langues*) and Use-languages (*langages*)

There are communities of use-language that cross the barriers of voice-language. I feel closer to the writers of the English- or Spanish-speaking Caribbean (or, of course, Creole-speaking) than to most writers of French. This is what makes us Antillean. Our voice-languages are different, our use-language (beginning with our relation to the voice-languages) is the same.

Literary genres.

As it strives toward totality, literary work moreover forms the ethnography of its own subject matter. We see a poem by Brathwaite as the equivalent of a novel by Carpentier and an essay by Fanon. We go even farther in not distinguishing between genres when we deny that their divisions are necessary for us or when we create different divisions.

Present moment and duration.

The two "realities" of time, whether it is considered to be linear, circular, cyclical, "natural," or "cultural." They determine the accents of our poetics. Might it be said that a poetics of the present moment would be blasphemous, while every poetics of duration would consecrate some unanimity?

## EXPANSE AND FILIATION

1. Daniel J. Boorstin, *The Discoverers: A History of Man's Search to Know His World and Himself* (New York: Random House, 1983), 201. *Trans.*

## CLOSED PLACE, OPEN WORD

1. This notion was expounded at length in *Eloge de la Créolité* by Jean Bernabé, Patrick Chamoiseau, and Raphael Confiant (Paris: Gallimard, 1989). The volume, dedicated in part to Glissant, proposes a transregional identity, history, and politics based on "creoleness"—a concept that, for Glissant, does not have the suppleness of process he finds in "creolization." *Trans.*
2. Saint-John Perse, *Eloges and other Poems*, Trans. Louise Varèse (New York: Bollingen/Pantheon, 1956), 17.
3. William Faulkner, *Intruder in the Dust* (New York: Random House, 1948). Interestingly, in the French translation, which Glissant has quoted here, this is far more explicit: "I do not know him in the least, and, as far as I know, there is no white man who does" (my translation of the French version). *Trans.*

215

4. Michael Dash, in his translation of Glissant's *Caribbean Discourse* (*Discours antillais*) (Charlottesville: University Press of Virginia, 1989), translates *détour* as *diversion* and *retour* as *reversion*. This is particularly interesting if one is attentive to the sense of *version*, thus, connecting it with an important meaning of Relation, i.e., "telling." I believe, however, that Glissant is vastly more interested in the movement implicit in both *détour* and *retour* and, therefore, translates these words as *detour* and *return*—or *go back*, etc., in the case of the latter. In this particular case, because noun and verb are identical in English, they convey more action—which action might, of course, be one of "diversion" or "distraction." See note 4 to the chapter "Errantry and Exile." *Trans.*

### CONCERNING THE POEM'S INFORMATION

1. The insertion of a text into a text, or the articulation of a part with a whole, sometimes will run counter to the overall economy. This reference to French critics who thus proclaim the end of poetry is only one relay for registering situations in the world, where poetry is on the increase as a means of expression.

### DICTATE, DECREE

1. Three related images of the world hypostasized by Glissant—*la totalité-monde*, *les échos-monde*, and *le chaos-monde*—have been left untranslated here, not only because of the inherent difficulty in translating them but also because they function as neologisms that have to be accepted into the French, so why not into English as well, since Glissant is working on languages in relation? Their structure cannot be duplicated in English. The article clearly modifies the first element (*la totalité*, *les échos*), but the second element (*monde*) is not a mere modifier, as it would appear to be if the normal English reversal of terms took place (i.e., world-totality, world-echoes, world-chaos). In fact, in this third instance all the implications of ordered chaos implicit in chaos theory would slip away, leaving the banality of world-disorder. Nor are these guises of the world (the world as totality, etc.); they are identities of the world. The world is totality,

216

echoes, and chaos, all at once, depending on our many ways of sensing and addressing it. *Trans.*

## TO BUILD THE TOWER

1. For Glissant, when these two words are set in contradistinction to each other, *langue* is the language one speaks and *langage* is how one speaks it. A *langue* may be a national language (French, Spanish, etc.) or an imposed language (French in Martinique) or a dominated language (Creole). A *langage* is a way of using language that can cross linguistic borders. Glissant shares a *langage* with writers who do not write in French: Derek Walcott, José Maria de Heredia, and Kamau Brathwaite, among others. In *Le Discours antillais* he described the relation between these two terms: "the Creole *langue*, which is natural to me, comes at every moment to irrigate my written practice of French, and my *langage* results from this symbiosis" (*DA*, 322; my translation). In *Caribbean Discourse* Michael Dash renders this distinction as "language" and "self-expression." It is perhaps an expression of Glissant's *langage* that he prefers to see the distinctions marked by composite words that indicate their fundamental connection; my translation of these words when they are set in this relation are language-voice (for *langue*) and language-use (for *langage*).

2. In *Le Discours antillais* I wrote: "I speak to you in your language-voice and I understand you in my language-use" (322). When all languages are equivalent, the poet's language-voice gives-on-and-with [*donne avec*] his language-use. For language-voice and language-use to be no longer differentiated presupposes that every language-voice has been set free as poetics. In the same way, to write is to experience oneself as already inhabited, in joyful nostalgia, by all the languages of the world.

## TRANSPARENCY AND OPACITY

1. Charaudeau's proposition concerning situational competence in the beginning student can be found in another form in an article by Robert B. Kaplan: "Cultural Thought Patterns in Inter-Cultural Education," *Language Learning* 16, nos. 1–2, 1–20. Kaplan examines the

217

conditions for teaching English as a second language in the United States. His general conclusion is that the foreign student, who has assimilated and mastered the rules perfectly, nonetheless is not immediately able to speak or write in the language: his or her situational competence—Kaplan doesn't use these words, but the idea is the same—needs to be developed by the teacher.

## THE RELATIVE AND CHAOS

1. It was when I was at UNESCO that the constant misunderstanding concerning these two senses of the word *culture* (among many others) became confirmed for me. Some of the Western officials who had served in this organization a long time were offended by the arrival of citizens from the countries of the south, seeing this as a sort of betrayal of the ideal of "culture" that, according to them, had governed its foundation. Going even further, they put the cultures of these countries, so obviously remote from what they considered to be humanistic accomplishment, in the same category as the various government regimes in charge of them. Barbarism, consequently, was penetrating the Institution, and you could hear these worthies grumbling to themselves: "Soon we'll be working under coconut palms." This mistake was two-pronged: "culture" was confused with humanistic sophistication, and people's cultures were confused with the governments ruling over them. Of course—and not to mention that there is little to choose between underdeveloped dictatorships in their sphere and many political regimes that are apparently much more civilized—it was not an innocent mistake.

   For, if they had been willing to consider that a culture is a totality, a participating *écho-monde*, by the same token they would have been willing to relinquish their exclusive privilege to "culture" and its administration. And, if they substantiated the notion that culture and government were equivalent, there was every possibility, or reason, to claim that this privilege should be maintained where it was, in the name of good "government of the things of this world."

   Arrangements of this sort met with approval from most of the representatives of the wealthy nations, which only allowed for supporting cultural assistance to poor countries on a selective basis (the only way they believed to be effective) and preferably in a bilateral context—in which fruitful negotiations were always possible.

Moreover, any global analysis of the situation—what UNESCO for a while summed up under the awkward title of "worldwide problematics"—was immediately pilloried by these representatives and declared useless or dangerous. Time and money wasted. It would, however, have been a major accomplishment on the part of an institution of that nature to have woven the beginnings of this global Relation.

Unfortunately, both the language conventions holding sway in such a context (particularly the punctilious precautions necessarily adopted to avoid shocking any of the parties involved) as well as the great number of reservations were significant curbs on this attempt, precisely at the point at which all the wealth of the imagination and of poetics should have been alerted. Poetics, in an international Organization!

The stubborn—it could be considered heroic—determination of Amadou-Mahtar M'Bow, the director general at the time, stemmed in large part from his conviction that it was in the interest of everyone, developed countries and countries in the process of development (as they were described), to try to define the global interdependency of problems and, consequently, that there was a multilateral necessity for solutions that might ensue from such an analysis. The affluent nations acknowledge no such joint interest. They are willing to distribute largesse but in proportion to friendly cooperation.

It is one of the phenomena of society that organs of the Western press seem to have constantly misinterpreted these facts. It is true that the heart of the debate was not meant to fascinate public opinion and that it is far more entertaining and more striking to pay attention to personalities or occasional conflicts presented in this manner. The flash-agents of the media (see n. 1 in the chapter "Distancing, Determining") performed their function here and concealed beneath pseudo-force lines ("Crisis at UNESCO!") the real ones. For example: "Preserve Freedom of the Press" obliterated the real issue: "Find a new equilibrium in the space of the world for the floods of information and their cultural cargo."

It was not an innocent mistake.

2. The terms *lieu commun* (common place) and *lieu-commun* (commonplace) are important for Glissant, and they are discussed at some length in the chapter "Relinked (Relayed), Related." Their English equivalents are less felicitous, perhaps, but *common place* can be

219

understood as the place common to coinciding cultures—the place they share—and *commonplace* exists in its commonplace sense as banality. *Trans.*

## DISTANCING, DETERMINING

1. *Flash agents* is my solution to Glissant's phrase "agents d'éclat." This term in French is no more instantly legible than my English phrase; generally, however, the function performed by these flash agents is defined by context. Constructed on the analogy of "press agents" (*agents de presse*), the formula goes beyond our very general notion of media to include a sense of instantaneous dazzlement wielded by hegemonic agents. *Trans.*

## RELINKED, (RELAYED), RELATED

1. In the French it is not clear that *langage* (use-language) is dominant in this case or that *langue* (voice-language) is dominated, but Glissant clarified this point for the translation. *Trans.*
2. One language's particularity—the addition in French of a hyphen (turning *lieu commun* [common place] into *lieu-commun* [commonplace]—allows me to venture a concept that goes beyond its occasion. This is something that would be impossible if sabirs replaced languages. Just think of the unimaginable reserves provided by the world's languages to produce just such ways of going beyond themselves. How many idioms, dialects, would we not take for inspiration to come back every time to mechanisms of Relation that cannot be dismantled? Failing to attain this multiplicity, we attempt to reach it from the very environment of the language in which we express ourselves. When we want to give-on-and-with multiplicity, we open the linguistic bastion and in turn multiply the language that we inhabit; we open stars into it: into a use-language that, by shortcutting, reassembles the language and scatters it.

## FOR OPACITY

1. *Comprehension* could, of course, be translated as "comprehension" to point out the root connection with the French word *comprendre*,

which I have earlier rendered as "to grasp" or, when the sense is mechanical, as "to comprehend" (and once, at Glissant's behest, as "to integrate"). In American English, however, the controlling attitude implied in this particular instance, vis-à-vis other people or cultures, is more apparent in *understanding* than in *comprehension. Trans.*

## OPEN CIRCLE, LIVED RELATION

1. Henri Meschonnic defines modernity by (among other things) a return of historicity. He thus seems to contradict the general current of structuralist thinking. But I sense—perhaps wrongly— that this historicity is abstracted from the evolution of the world. We are summoned not so much by historicity as by the diffracted synchronicity of peoples' histories. The active presence of these peoples is what antihistorical thought has mutely impugned with its self-defensive tactics. Historicity takes place only in liberated geographies.

Meschonnic, for example, deplores the excessive use in contemporary critical texts, of the word *horizon.* No doubt because he suspects there is a project there, the intention of conquest (one more arrow-like nomadism), the breakthrough of an ideology or—coming down to the same thing—of a propagating ideal. The word *horizon* loses this meaning, however, when it is a question of the realized horizon of the world. Would not modernity be the contradictory and reflected totality of cultures? The horizon is how all these places circle the planet. Though, in the meanwhile, humanity is updating all over again, in a deplorable manner, the old understanding and usage of this word, by "projecting" against yet unimaginable places, to the interplanetary horizon.

Perhaps modernity exists when a tradition functioning in a time and place no longer gradually assimilates the changes offered, either from within or from without, but adapts to them by violence. Violence does not in every instance mean a break, which could emerge latently. But, because the violence of change has become widespread these days and increased its speed, it can be described as absolutely modern.

Thus, sequences of modernity have laid the groundwork for modernity. And the latter, extravagant and endogenous, is consumed in its predicates. Its duration is its extremity: the more modernity is flaunted, the more it is unrealized. Following this logic, one could think of successive futures without modernity or of infinite modernities with no future.

What Western cultures call the postmodern is an attempt to find an order in (and put some order into) this reality that is experienced as chaos, without, however, abandoning the energy of this chaos. An attempt to manage modernity by putting it in order. In other words, anchoring oneself the best one can in the continuum of one's own production. That is, indeed, one of the most obvious temptations of postmodernism, which takes as its subject the formalist resurrection of the works and ornaments of the Western past, adapted to the current magma. But, as we have previously suggested on several occasions, aesthetic and philosophical thoughts, no matter which culture engendered them, will have to break away from the birth of their own history alone, to give-on-and-with every possible contamination. They will have to implement their Other of thought. Currently, there are no signs of any appreciable beginnings of these self-breaks. Except perhaps in the West, and as if by antiphrasis, the intellectual quest for an *epistemological break,* whatever it may be and wherever it is brought to bear, is evidence of a feeling for (but also of a resentment against) this need to break with the exclusivity of one's continuum.

2. Generalization has brought about some dramatic moments on the planet.

Leon Trotsky's symbolic figure hovered over the drama of the dispersal of Trotskyite intelligences and generosities.

Stalinism, by taking the Revolution back into a single country, reactivated the generalizing universal—always ethnocentric and absolute. The Third International was the tragic instrument of this generalization.

Trotskyism, developing the theory of permanent Revolution, attempted to escape this generalizing universal and to replace it with a concrete and relativized universal.

But the liberations of nations cannot be programmed in a universal manner. The Trotskyist perspective, which freed the lessons of Marxism from the straitjacket of State nationalism, did not go far enough in its evolution.

Today we know that Marxist philosophy (or the philosophy of Marx) was, like all philosophies of History, linear (one History, one driving force: the class struggle; an agent: the proletariat; an end: classless society) and ethnocentric (it moved from the outermost parts of the world toward the great cities of Europe). But it also took its strength from an imaginary structure that had to have been its first inspiration and that, beyond theory, presented the world as a totality.

The idea of permanent Revolution, if it were to radiate outward in contradiction, could not be merely ideological. It is the a priori (the programmable calendar of liberation movements) one would have had to go beyond in order to appreciate the extent to which Marxist thought had contributed methodological progress in grasping situations. This thought contained seeds of the generalizing universal: it authorized the Stalinist monstrosities. Whereas the Marxist imaginary, if it had been separated from its obsession with seizing power, would have had the opposite effect, providing for Relation.

Trotskyism went farther, but its tragedy lay in not making a systematic criticism of Stalinist ethnocentrism and not applying some of this critique to Marxist theory itself, at least as this theory was interpreted by the Russian revolutionaries.

This is why Trotskyism ran into the stubborn particularities of specific situations just about everywhere, in a dust of heroic, ridiculous, and usually vague battles.

That's all easy to say—and quickly said—today.

But it is true that this was an abortive *écho-monde* that left deep in many the grip of regret and nostalgia.

3. Among these binarities, whether or not they can be transcended:

Matrix abyss, immeasurable abyss.
Arrowlike nomadism: —circular nomadism.
Discovery, Conquest.
Linearity—circularity.
Filiation—extension.
Legitimacy—contingency.
Center: —peripheries.
Differences: singularities.
Transparency—opacity.
Generalization—generality.
(Faulkner, Saint-John Perse.)
Classicisms—Baroque.

Models—*Echos-monde.*
Relative: Chaos.
Totality: Relation.
Grasping (*comprendre*)—giving-on-and-with (*donner avec*).
Sense (in linear terms), the full-sense (in circularity).
Aesthetics of the universe: aesthetics of Chaos.
Voice languages: use-languages.
Writing: orality.
The instant, duration.
History—histories.
Root identity—relation identity.
Thought of the Other: —the Other of thought.
Assimilations—distancings that determine.
Relinked (relayed), Related.
Relay agents—flash agents.
Common place: commonplace.
Violence, deculturation.
Creolizations, errantry.

In this litany commas (,) indicate relation, dashes (—) opposition, and colons (:) consecution.

# References

Is it not one of the conditions of writing today that it conceive of itself as preceded by a pretext of discourse? In any case, this is what usually happens: I accept invitations to expose my points of view publicly whenever the proposed conference fits in with my (nonprojectile) project. And sometimes the suggested theme will have a ripple effect, set rootlets, or swerve in some new direction.

The public lecture functions as a sort of first draft to the written text resulting from it. But this presentation will have determined, meanwhile, the lineages of the text and oriented its economy. The practice of writing then will tighten, or draw out, what the lecture brought to light. Preliminary written texts sometimes function in this process as approaches that foretell and really provoke orality.

These two practices contribute to a phenomenon that is no longer certifiably either "pure" writing or transcribed orality. The consequence of this is that, with each edition of such a text, if there happen to be any, the temptation arises (by recalling these relayed techniques) to change—to perfect?—the letter of it, over and over again. What is related thus varies (at the same time that the substance of Relation moves) toward a perfectibility of expression that does not arrive at an absolute. To what extremities can this go? What is the limit? No doubt to the point where voice begins to fail and the hand stops.

The following are some of the occasions that have preceded (sometimes authorized) the work of overall elaboration for this volume.

"The Open Boat" (La Barque ouverte). Paper for the colloquium "L'experience du gouffre" (Experience of the Abyss), Louvain, 1986.

"Errantry, Exile" (L'errance, l'exil). Lecture given in 1987 as part of a series on "L'errance," in Martinique.

"Poetics" (Poétiques). A synthesis of two sets of observations given as separate lectures at Temple University (Philadelphia) and Rice University (Houston) in 1988 and 1989. The final text was presented at the University of California at Berkeley in March 1990.

"A Rooted Errantry" (Une errance enracinée). The first version appeared as the preface to "Pour Saint-John Perse," published by GEREC (Groupe d'études et de recherches créolophones), Martinique, 1988.

"Closed Place, Open Word" (Lieu clos, parole ouverte). Given at the Colloquium on the Plantation system, Center for French and Francophone Studies, Louisiana State University (Baton Rouge), April 1989.

"Concerning a Baroque Abroad in the World" (D'un baroque mondialisé) and "To Build the Tower" (Bâtir la tour) were reworked from texts that appeared in *Le courrier de l'Unesco,* 1985 and 1986.

"Concerning the Poem's Information" (De l'information du poème) was first approached at the colloquium "Poésie et informatique," Liège, 1984.

"Transparency and Opacity" (Transparence et opacité). Theme developed before the Congress of French Professors of South America, Bogotá, 1982.

"The Relative and Chaos" (Le relatif et le chaos) is based on a paper given before the Association of Professors of Physical Chemistry of Martinique, 1980.

"Distancing, Determining" (Les écarts déterminants). Presented at a meeting of l'Assaupamar (Association pour la Sauvegarde du Patrimoine Martiniquais), August 1989.